A Small Matter of Programming

A Small Matter of Programming
Perspectives on End User Computing

Bonnie A. Nardi

The MIT Press
Cambridge, Massachusetts
London, England

Second printing, 1995

© 1993 Massachusetts Institute of Technology

This book was set in Sabon by TechBooks and was printed and bound in the United States of America.

Library of Congress Cataloging-in-Publication Data

Nardi, Bonnie A.
    A small matter of programming : perspectives on end user computing
    Bonnie A. Nardi.
        p.   cm.
    Includes bibliographical references and index.
    ISBN 0-262-14053-5
    1. End-user computing. 2. Programming (Electronic computers)
I. Title.
QA76.9.E53N37   1993
005.1—dc20   93-9124
                                                                        CIP

This book is dedicated to Anthony, Christopher, and Jeanette

Contents

Figures

Preface

"It's only a small matter of programming . . . "

In the programming community, one often hears this epigrammatic comment following a lengthy technical discussion of some difficult problem of software design. The comment typically provokes smiles—every irony is intended by the speaker—and the speaker is understood to mean:

- To solve the difficult problem, there is a lot of work to be done.
- It looks like it's doable, but the difficulties that will inevitably arise are impossible to predict and could be a lot more serious than we now imagine.
- We are programmers, so of course we can solve this problem.

The comment helps move the software project along its natural path by signifying that the time for action has come—the business of programming is at hand. For end users, the time for programming has come also—end users can do much more than draw pictures or process documents or maintain calendars with computers. This book asks why it has been so difficult for end users to command programming power and explores the critical problems of end user application development that must be solved to afford end users greater computational power.

There is a tremendous demand for the ability to create, customize, specialize, and extend software applications. End users want these capabilities; they have the detailed task knowledge necessary for creating the knowledge-rich applications they want and the motivation to get their work done quickly, to a high standard of accuracy and completeness. We know that end users can be empowered to build their own applications—often surprisingly sophisticated applications—because of more than a decade of widespread use of application development environments such as spreadsheets, statistical packages, and CAD systems.

What spreadsheets, statistical packages, and CAD systems have in common is a carefully chosen set of task-specific operations that allow programming within a particular set of tasks. They lack the power of general programming languages, but they also lack the steep learning curve—hence they are much better suited to the needs of users who have little or no training in computer science, and often little interest in computers *per se*. Most end users regard computers as useful—even indispensable—machines capable of helping them work more productively, creatively, and with greater pleasure. This is not the same as finding computers themselves intrinsically interesting—as a computer scientist or engineer would—and it dictates an entirely different set of tools for end users.

Spreadsheets, statistical packages, and CAD systems have survived in the cutthroat world of software sales because they serve large constituencies, and serve them well. However, there is enormous untapped potential to use computers productively for end user application development environments that would serve smaller, more specialized, but nevertheless highly critical problem areas such as patient care, library management, scientific collaboration, and a wide variety of educational simulation systems, to name but a very few. While programmers can be called in to provide applications for users in such areas, once the software is written, users are stuck with the applications given them by programmers, and the applications cannot easily be changed, extended, or tailored to meet the demands of local conditions. In addition to the lack of flexibility of delivered applications, users will have paid a lot for the application, and they will have spent much time transferring their domain knowledge to the programmer to get the application written at all. A patient record system, for example, that works well in one hospital might need modifications or extensions to work well in another hospital, or even in different units within the same hospital. End users, who understand the particulars of their own areas, should be able to make such modifications and extensions. Users may also be starting new applications afresh, as users of spreadsheets, CAD systems, and statistical packages routinely do.

The chief problems to be solved in providing more end user application development environments are (1) to provide highly specialized end user programming environments that leverage users' existing task-related interests and skills, and (2) from an organizational perspective, to reorganize work practices to better support end users. How are we to do these things? That is the subject of this book, and there is much to convince you, the reader, of before we can arrive at a set of common understandings about the nature of end user programming and the solutions to the problems of end user computing proposed in this book. To achieve that understanding, we explore three key areas:

• Task-specific programming languages
• Visual application frameworks
• Collaborative work practices

The differing threads of these discussions are developed to expose and analyze issues in end user computing by casting a wide net, taking a careful look at the social and cognitive dimensions of computer use, as well as more narrowly technical subjects. To presage, in the briefest terms, what we will ultimately be leading up to: end users will freely write their own applications when they have task-specific programming languages embedded in appropriate visual frameworks, and they will write applications in collaboration with other users. There is much to say before that last cryptic statement makes much sense, and so, let us turn our attention to the fascinating and difficult issues of end user computing. With any luck, it will be only a small matter of programming to make the dream of a profusion of highly specialized, task-specific end user computing environments an everyday reality.

Acknowledgments

Many people contributed ideas, enthusiasm, and practical advice to the writing of this book. The Application Architectures Project in the former Human-Computer Interaction Department at Hewlett-Packard Labs in Palo Alto was my home for the work described herein. Special thanks go to Jim Miller, our project manager, and Jeff Johnson and Craig Zarmer, my fellow project members. Nancy Kendzierski, our department manager, supported our work for the duration of our three-year project.

Many people commented on individual chapters in the book, or provided helpful discussion on points I was thinking through: Lucy Berlin, Betsy Brenner, Susan Brennan, Chee Chew, Dave Duis, Danielle Fafchamps, Walt Hill, Thomas Green, Martin Griss, Robin Jeffries, Andreas Paepcke, Jasmina Pavlin, Vicki O'Day, Darrell Raymond, and anonymous reviewers. Michelle Gantt coauthored the CHI '92 paper of which chapter 6 is an expanded version. Nick Rousseau coauthored the Human-Computer Interaction paper of which chapter 4 is an expanded version. My collaborations with them were most enjoyable.

Bob Prior and the congenial staff at MIT Press helped to move this project along quickly and provided just the right level of prodding and practical help to enable me to complete the book on schedule.

In the spirit of collaborative programming, Mike Lemon and Andreas Paepcke provided me with programs and help with the used to produce the manuscript. The wizardry of the HPLabs Research Library staff was a tremendous boon to the research for the book.

Many thanks to my husband, Chris Darrouzet, for conversation and companionship, and for his support in encouraging me to write this book.

My sons' unselfconscious facility with computers gives me gut level assurance that end user computing is an important part of our future. It is my hope that my infant daughter and her cohorts will have much more accessible technology than we have today, and this book is intended to be a small contribution in that direction.

Finally, I owe a debt of gratitude to those who participated in the empirical studies. They must remain anonymous, and the time they unselfishly devoted to the research has been duly entered, I hope, on the credit side of the great cosmic ledger of human decency. The thoughtfulness, reflection, and wit with which study participants answered questions and managed to inform me of information I didn't even know I needed made the empirical research a special pleasure.

1

Introduction

Literacy was not widespread in Mesopotamia. The scribes ... had to undergo training, and having completed their training and become entitled to call themselves dubsar, *"scribe," they were members of a privileged elite who might look with contempt on their fellow citizens.*

—C. B. F. Walker, *Cuneiform*

Futuristic scenarios of end user computing often reveal the computer as an intelligent "agent" capable of performing actions inferred from a simple statement such as we might issue to a human assistant. The human assistant is valued because he can,[1] on his own, break a task down into its constituent parts, correctly anticipate next steps, and fill in missing details. The hope is that the computer will be able to do the same. An example of the computer-as-agent scenario is offered by Tesler in *Scientific American* (1991). He suggests that the computer will be able to respond to an instruction such as: "Distribute this draft to the rest of the group and let me know when they've read it." Such a request involves considerable planning and coordination, but intelligent agents will be able to perform the appropriate actions because "programmers will ... endow [agents] with ... reasoning capabilities." These capabilities are to be very sophisticated, including the ability to "anticipate needs before the user has expressed them or has even become aware of them." The impending availability of computer assistants/agents amounts to nothing less than a "paradigm shift" in which the computer has changed from "cloistered oracle to personal implement to active assistant" (Tesler 1991).

Tesler, of course, is not the only one to project the computer-as-agent scenario. The lineage of such scenarios is long, going back through many incarnations in science fiction, attaining world fame with HAL, the temperamental computer-agent in the film *2001: A Space Odyssey*, and continuing on in the *Knowledge Navigator* and *1995* videos produced by Apple Computer and Hewlett-Packard, respectively. What interests me about these scenarios is not that they make fantastic, unrealistic promises (though I think they do), or that the instructions given by the user are couched in simple English (Tesler at least concedes that more structured languages may be needed), or that they embody such a grand vision (though the vision has much appeal). Rather, it is interesting that it is the *programmer* who is to control all of the computational magic. As Tesler says, *programmers* will endow computer-agents with their basic capabilities, even meeting such exciting challenges as programming the computer to know what users will think before they think it! By comparison, notice the relationship of the end user to the computer; the end user is engaged in the most humdrum activities: making queries regarding a phone conversation, asking the computer to set up an appointment, requesting articles from the library (Tesler, 1991).

Now contrast this vision of the computer-agent with what Alan Kay (in the same issue of *Scientific American*) envisions for educational software: children writing simulations of complex natural phenomena such as biological and physical systems to better understand how they function. Kay's colleagues have created a simulation construction kit for children so that they can build their own simulations. The construction kit lets children write simple scripts that model animal behavior. Using the kit they can change parameters to see how changing conditions affect the animal. This use of computers is an instance of what Tesler called the "personal implement": the children are doing nothing more or less than *programming*. With the kit, the children have tools that give them tremendous scope for intellectual exploration and personal empowerment. Kay reported that the children have, with much enthusiasm, simulated an unusual animal, the clown fish, "produc[ing] simulations that reflect how the fish acts when it gets hungry, seeks food, acclimates to an anemone, and escapes from predators" (Kay, 1991).

There is an intellectual richness here that is missing from the utilitarian scenarios emanating from the agent metaphor. The richness derives directly from the ability of the children to program the computer. I am concerned that in our zeal to move on to the "next paradigm" we may be missing a tremendous opportunity to extend and deepen the current paradigm. We have only scratched the surface of what would be possible if end users could freely program their own applications, as the children have done. In fact, such an ability would itself constitute a new paradigm. We may indeed want to turn over some functions to computer agents, but let us also open up the world of programming to end users. As has been shown time and again, no matter how much designers and programmers try to anticipate and provide for what users will need, the effort always falls short because it is impossible to know in advance what may be needed. Customizations, extensions, and new applications become necessary. End users should have the ability to create these customizations, extensions, and applications, just as the school children chose to explore the behavior of the clown fish using the simulation construction kit. Next the children may want to study herring gulls or mountain gorillas or European honeybees, and their programming resources and newly formed programming skills will enable them to do so. While computer agents will be appropriate and useful for many tasks, such agents do not begin to cover the extent of what end users will be able to do with computers when they have suitable environments for creating their own applications. We should be working on many fronts, and agents and implements and even oracles all have their place in the world of computing.

Dunlop and Kling (1991) write that our technical choices advance social goals. The goal we seek to advance here is that of giving more direct control over computational resources to end users, to enable them to do with computers what professional programmers have long done. The goal is practical: to encourage the proliferation of end user programming environments that will give ordinary users some of the computational power enjoyed by professional programmers, so that they can perform their work more efficiently, effectively, and pleasurably. In meeting this simple, practical goal, we may also hope to serve the higher goal of educating people about the way computers work: through practical experience, the nature of the machine—its possibilities and limits—can be studied and reflected upon in the course of everyday activity. Such exposure to computers does not guarantee more informed understanding, but it at least permits it, so that the many decisions a democratic society faces about the use of computers, including difficult issues of privacy, freedom of speech, and civil liberties, can be approached by ordinary citizens from a more knowledgeable standpoint.

In addition to supporting a populist vision of computing, a focus on end user programming addresses the problem of the serious underutilization of computing resources that has begun to trouble many observers. Forester (1989) noted that there is a "new wave of skepticism" regarding the productivity benefits of automation. Many studies suggest that the introduction of computers into offices and factories has not generally correlated with increased productivity (Bowen, 1989; Franke, 1989; Shaiken, 1989; Warner, 1989; Strassman, 1990). Forester calls this the "productivity puzzle."

There are many complex reasons why automation has not produced the expected productivity gains. The puzzle has many pieces, including some that have nothing whatsoever to do with technology. In particular, a net decline in productivity can occur when countervailing forces (e.g., the need for increased legal and personnel staff to monitor government regulations and employee entitlements) depress productivity more than automation, which is contributing to productivity, can increase it. But even taking this into account, we do seem to be underutilizing our technology (Bowen, 1989). One key reason for this underutilization is the pyramid of computers users: a broad base of potential end users with a tiny point of professional programmers. Because of the expense of engaging professional programmers to create applications from specifications, many end users never get the applications they want, and their computers sit on the desktop gathering dust, or are used only for a narrow range of applications, such as word processing. The *1990 Software Market Survey* reported that the average corporate application development backlog in 1990 was twenty-nine months (*Software Magazine, 1990*). Such figures, alarming as they are, count only the applications that people have actually requested, not those that they might want if they were not working in an environment of such overwhelmingly unsatisfied demand. When end users can create their own applications and do not have to rely exclusively on MIS departments, consultants, and others to create their applications, existing computational resources will become much more valuable and will begin to justify their cost.

JUST WHO ARE END USERS?

A user of a software system was heard to remark, "I didn't have much time, so I did it the long way." In this statement we hear the authentic voice of the end user: the person who does not want to turn a task into a programming problem, who would rather follow a lengthy but well-known set of procedures to get the job done. The converse of this statement, putatively from a collection of MIT graffiti, goes: "I would rather write programs to help me write programs than write programs."[2]

These two users define the endpoints of a continuum of computer users. It is helpful to understand that a key difference between professional programmers and end users is that programmers like computers because they get to program, and end users like computers because they get to get their work done. End users are not "casual," "novice," or "naive" users; they are people such as chemists, librarians, teachers, architects, and accountants, who have computational needs and want to make serious use of computers, but who are not interested in becoming professional programmers. Many such users use computers daily, at least for certain periods of intensive work on a project. The development of end user systems should be targeted at these users; people with infrequent computational needs can enlist contract programmers or in-house programmers to write the few programs they will need.

JUST WHAT IS END USER PROGRAMMING?

There are many systems that could conceivably fall under the rubric of "end user programming systems." In this book we are concerned with systems such as spreadsheets, CAD systems, and statistical packages, which allow end users to create useful applications with no more than a few hours of instruction. In an end user programming system, a critical subset of the functionality of the system can be quickly learned and is sufficient for getting useful work done.

Before we go any further, we must say what we mean by "programming." There are two ways to approach the problem. We can define programming as a behavior in which sequences of procedural instructions (typically in textual format) are written in a language that is compiled or interpreted into the application. Thus, we may hear marketing people claim that fourth-generation languages (4GLs) do not require programming because of the declarative nature of the specifications. However, we would suggest that writing high level, declarative, textual program specifications also constitutes programming, as does creating diagrammatic representations of system behavior. They demand the same basic activities and skills as conventional programming (even if the programmer is saved a considerable amount of time). The point is that a definition of programming that refers to detailed behavior is likely to be technology-specific.

If we attempt to define programming by its objective, we can address many related technologies that are of importance to end users. The objective of programming is to create an application that serves some function for the user. From the end user's point of view, the particular behavior involved is not important, so long as application development is easy and relatively rapid. In this respect, we can include automatic programming systems, programming by example systems, and form-filling dialogues in which applications can be customized. Figure 1.1, as rough as it is, suggests a continuum of programmability in which parameter setting and traditional programming form the ends of the continuum.

THE EMPIRICAL STUDIES

The ideas in this book have evolved from two empirical studies of end user computing: a study of spreadsheet users (Nardi and Miller, 1990; 1991; Nardi and Zarmer, 1991) and a study of CAD users (Gantt and Nardi, 1992). The motivation for the empirical studies was to find out what kinds of successful end user programming systems are in actual use and to learn what makes them successful. We believe that there are generalizable lessons that can be learned from successful systems and applied to the design of new software systems—as well as to new social systems to support effective software use. Of course design still is, and almost certainly always will be, a black art whose most crucial elements remain an incalculable mix of imagination, intuition, and intellectual interaction with one's fellows. Empirical studies are not a "turn-the-crank" panacea to the problems of design; designs do not flow directly from studies of users. Rather, empirical studies are intended to create an atmosphere in which the actual experiences of users become a part of the discourse of

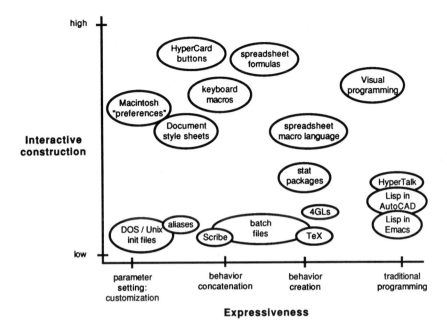

Figure 1.1
Programmable systems

design. This discourse may take on a very specific flavor; this book, for example, makes specific suggestions for the design of end user programming languages, environments, and the social organization needed to support end user programming. The intent of empirical studies as a part of the design process is to provide a stimulus to creativity, not to assume that design can be programmatically directed. A close examination of the actual experiences of successful users can provide a useful point of departure for designers, suggesting new perspectives from which to view the artifacts they create.

The empirical studies described here were naturalistic, ethnographic studies with a small number of users. The goal was to achieve an in-depth understanding of the everyday use of the software systems studied, rather than to test specific hypotheses with statistical methods. An advantage of the ethnographic approach is that it is exploratory in nature, leaving open the possibility of finding interesting but unanticipated phenomena. Indeed, we were surprised at some of what we found in the spreadsheet and CAD studies; in particular, our findings on the collaborative nature of end user application development were completely unanticipated.[3] Our questions (see Appendix) were adjusted after a few interviews as it became obvious that we needed to pay attention to cooperative work practices.

Several key activities comprised the ethnographic research. We conducted in-depth interviews with informants[4] (eleven spreadsheet users and twenty-four CAD users); collected and analyzed informants' artifacts (e.g., floppies with spreadsheet applications; printouts of macro programs, spreadsheets, slides; and plotted CAD designs); and studied and used the software systems of interest (VisiCalc, Lotus 1-2-3, and Microsoft Excel for spreadsheets; and HP ME30 for CAD).[5]

Informants were found through an informal process of referral. Interviews were tape-recorded in informants' offices or work settings. A set of open-ended questions was asked of each informant in the course of the interview (see Appendix). We discussed users' tasks, how they used the software system to accomplish them, and how use of the system fit into the overall workflow. The order of the questions varied depending on the course of the conversation. Additional conversational leads were followed as they arose. Informants showed us examples of their work on-screen and in paper form. Approximately seven hundred pages of transcribed material resulted from the interviews across the two studies.

In the spreadsheet study, informants were college-educated people employed in diverse companies, from small start-ups to large corporations of several thousand employees. They had varying degrees of computer experience, ranging from someone who only recently learned to use a computer to professional programmers. Most had no computer science background and three to five years experience with spreadsheets. Users' applications were in either financial or engineering domains.

In the CAD study, informants included architects, mechanical engineers, electrical engineers, and industrial designers. They came from seven companies, ranging from a three-person architecture design office to Fortune 100 companies. Most informants had college degrees, and all had at least two years of college. Most had been using CAD for at least five years. Informants' computer experience ranged from those who were completely self-taught to one engineer with a degree in computer science (and a degree in electrical engineering). Most informants had taken some formal programming or product classes. Many had also put in long hours studying on their own. Our study focused on commercially available CAD systems rather than proprietary custom systems.

Occasionally we provide verbatim quotations from users in the studies to illustrate a point. Where user names are given, they are fictitious.

SO MUCH YET TO DO ...

We rely heavily on our spreadsheet and CAD studies in this book because there are few in-depth empirical studies of the actual use of end user programming systems, and because these systems are pervasive and indisputably successful. Many existing empirical studies focus only on small aspects of a system; for example, among spreadsheet studies, Olson and Nilsen (1987) conducted an experiment in which they contrasted the methods by which subjects entered formulas in two different spreadsheet products, and Brown and Gould (1987) counted mistakes made during an experimental trial of spreadsheet use (see also Napier et al., 1989; Doyle, 1990). In addition to our own work, we have relied on the empirical studies of Clement (1990), Mackay (1990a), MacLean et al., (1990), T. R. G. Green and his colleagues, Rousseau (1992a; 1992b), Tee (1992) and others. One hope for this book is that it will stimulate further empirical research on existing end user software systems so that we can learn more about what works and what doesn't work. Over the last twenty years or so, computer access has slowly been extended to less sophisticated users, and there is much to be learned from studying the successes and failures of programmable systems that have large user populations. It would be enlightening to know more about user experience with systems such as statistical packages, 4GLs, style sheets in word processing programs, HyperCard, Metaphor Capsules, and Mathematica.[6] At the moment, a simple diagram such as figure 1.1 cannot be drawn with the level of assurance we would like, given our current level of knowledge, but ideally we would like to know enough to be able to represent knowledge about the dimensions of various programming systems in such schematic form.

OVERVIEW

The subject of this book is the study of technologies designed to support *complete end user application development*, not technologies that support only part of the development process such as the creation of user inter-faces, specifications, or throwaway prototypes. While there is a place for activities such as rapid prototyping and user interface building, these ap-proaches do not enable end users to build their own finished applications. These approaches may be useful in getting end users involved in the de-sign process, but they are not the direct support for end user application development which is our goal.

We begin, in chapter 2, by asking why we need end user programming systems at all. Aren't natural language-based systems that will allow us to just tell the computer what we want right around the corner? We discuss the computer's conversational abilities and argue that conversation is not the best model for human-computer communication.

Instead of conversation, we propose that human-computer communi-cation is best facilitated by *task-specific programming languages* that tap users' task knowledge and related interests. Chapter 3 describes the kinds of programming languages that will support end user programming. The argument is made that people readily learn formal languages, and that what end users need are task-specific languages that exploit existing task understanding.

Much work on end user programming has concentrated on specific in-teractional techniques that have been proposed as general solutions to problems of end user computing. These techniques include forms-based systems, visual languages, programming by example, programming by example modification, and automatic program generation. Chapter 4 ex-plains and evaluates these techniques.

Chapter 5 proposes the development of visual application frameworks for end user computing. The model is the spreadsheet table, which visually organizes computation.

Our empirical studies convinced us that to understand end user pro-gramming, it is critical to attend to both the use of a software product by an individual user and the collaborative work practices that accom-pany the use of the software. A narrow focus on individual cognition that accounts only for the individual's interaction with a particular soft-ware system misses much of what is critical to application development. In particular, we have found that software systems afford users more power—but not at the expense of ease of use—when collaborative work practices are employed. As we describe in chapter 6, the work of building an application is distributed over different kinds of users whose varying skills and interests are marshaled to get the application written.

Finally, in chapter 7 we look at a software system that is intended to facilitate the process of creating task-specific end user programming systems. The cost of building many such systems will be prohibitively high unless we provide a firm foundation of reusable software components that ease the development process.

2

Conversation and Computers

By degrees I made a discovery of still greater moment. I found that . . . people possessed a method of communicating their experience and feelings to one another by articulate sounds. I perceived that the words they spoke sometimes produced pleasure or pain, smiles or sadness, in the minds and countenances of hearers. This was indeed a godlike science, and I ardently desired to become acquainted with it. But I was baffled in every attempt I made for this purpose.

—Frankenstein's monster, *Frankenstein*, by Mary Shelley

Before we examine end user computing languages, environments, and work practices, we must ask why it is that people need these things anyway—why can't we just tell computers what to do using a simple conversational style of communication? Researchers have been promising for quite some time that very soon . . . any day now . . . communicating with computers won't be a problem because we will just talk to them the way we talk to one another. If this were to happen, the entire problem of end user programming would vanish.

While there are certainly applications for which a conversation-like user interface to the computer would be useful, in general this approach is problematic for the kind of complex communication demanded by end user application development. The difficulty lies in the fact that while humans effortlessly, unselfconsciously converse as an unproblematic matter of everyday life, computers are, quite literally, unable to hold up their end of the conversation. The reasons for the computer's conversational deficiencies inhere in the very nature of conversation itself, as we shall see.

MIMICKING CONVERSATION

A pervasive assumption about human-computer communication is that ideally it should mimic human conversation. More specifically, it should mimic ordinary, mundane conversation[1] such as a chat between friends. This assumption informs many conceptualizations of how people should interact with computers, from marketing videos (*Knowledge Navigator* and *1995*) to serious scholarly treatments of the problems of human-machine communication (Chapanis, 1975; Hayes and Reddy, 1983; Bolt, 1984; Suchman, 1987; Norman and Thomas, 1990; Robinson, 1990). Suchman (1987), for example, calls informal conversation "the paradigm case" for communication.

Conversation has a number of obvious advantages as a model for human-computer interaction. Most importantly, we already know how to talk, so no new learning is necessary. Conversation provides a rich, expressive communication channel; it is the main way that we coordinate our activities, share information, and maintain human relationships. Given the central place of conversation in human life, it does appear to offer a good model for human-computer communication.

But there is a problem. Unlike Frankenstein's monster, who, despite his monstrousness, had a human intelligence, and who did, through "great application," go on to master the godlike science, computers have remained quite stubbornly resistant to our continuing efforts to endow them with the ability to carry on conversations. At most we have been able to write programs that allow computers to understand a limited range of "natural language" within a set of narrowly bounded tasks, such as making airline reservations. To do even this much requires massive amounts of programming, and of course the computer understands only a subset of the sentences that might meaningfully be used to do a task. Rich (1985) notes that in natural language systems, "users must learn not the interface language itself, from scratch, but rather the boundaries that sit within a language that they already know and that divide the recognizable sublanguage from the rest of the natural language." So the learning problem does not disappear; it takes shape as the problem of learning a sublanguage.

The biggest stumbling block to human-computer communication via natural language lies in the nature of conversation itself. The computer fails to understand and to speak because much of what is understood in a conversation attaches to the *context* in which the participants of a conversation find themselves, and of which they have knowledge. People bring a great fund of prior knowledge to a conversation, which they use to interpret what they hear and to determine what they say. People are also continually monitoring the situation in which they find themselves through the five senses (Schutz 1962, 1964; Garfinkel, 1967) to gain knowledge of the referents and meanings of the conversation—referents and meanings that may be only barely sketched in as far as the actual words of a sentence go. For example, a grocery shopper standing over the lettuce bin, to use a scenario offered by Heritage (1984), may remark to another shopper: "That's a nice one." The referent for "that's" is a lettuce; the word "nice" takes its meaning strictly from the context of the particular shopping event being enacted by the shoppers, a context in which the characteristics of a particular lettuce are at issue. In a different conversational context, "That's a nice one" might come to be construed quite differently. A Halloween partygoer, for example, standing around with her friends, admiring others' costumes, might exclaim, "That's a nice one!" In this situation, "that's" refers to a costume, and "nice" might be used to describe a particularly macabre getup. "Nice" then, can mean something like "fresh and green" in one context, and "scary and sinister" in another. (See also Grice, 1975 and Levinson, 1983.) These widely varying referents and meanings cause no trouble at all to the participants in the conversation; they bring to bear a full range of knowledge and perceptions in producing and understanding conversation.

The accomplishment of conversation, then, relies on a large and difficult-to-specify cache of prior knowledge, as well as an ability to perceive the environment through the senses. The computer lacks these capabilities, so while the production and comprehension of conversation function well in human communication because a context can be established, the computer fails miserably at conversation. Lacking the critical resources necessary for conversation, the computer can neither understand nor speak. (See Suchman, 1987 on these points. Winograd and Flores, 1986 also treat these issues against a philosophical backdrop.)

That conversation requires capabilities absent in the computer should not occasion dismay as far as our efforts in designing systems of human-computer communication go; it simply means that we need another model of human-computer interaction. There is much resistance, however, to the idea that we give up the conversational model. The computer is our creation, and we have endowed it with so many amazing abilities that giving it speech and understanding seems only a matter of hard work. The computer's humanoid intelligence fairly cries out for this essential missing ability.[2] In addition, the central importance of conversation in human communication causes us to be a bit myopic when imagining how we want to communicate with computers: the computer must communicate the way we do, or, more precisely, the way that we think we communicate most readily, that is, via ordinary conversation. Because conversation dominates our daily communicative activities, it overshadows the many other ways we communicate—ways that might provide more suitable models for human-computer communication. For example, Winograd and Flores (1986) note that, "[Driving a car] is not achieved by having a car communicate like a person [i.e., through conversation], but by providing *the right coupling between the driver and action in the relevant domain* (motion down the road)" (emphasis added).

To play a piece of music, to take another example, we read the score. An important communicative event has occurred over what may have been a great deal of time and space. The communication stretches from composer to player via the musical notation, and, though we do not usually draw this fact to our conscious awareness, significant communication has been effected through a formal language in which musical parameters and events are symbolically recorded (see Hutchins, 1987). Reading music is quite unlike carrying on a conversation, but it serves the task of playing a piece of music and involves significant communication.

COMMUNICATION AS A PRACTICAL ACTIVITY

Mundane conversation is actively, consciously produced daily; it feels immediate, fruitful, like what "communication" is all about. Thus we tend to accept mundane conversation as the most natural model of communication, as "the paradigm case." What we need to do, however, is to look carefully at the particular goals, constraints, and resources brought to the communicative setting by all parties to the communication. Unfortunately many researchers have made the assumption that *conversation* is synonymous with *informal, mundane conversation*, that mundane conversation should be taken as exemplary. Many conversation analysts argue that mundane conversation is the primary, even "primordial" way humans communicate (Goodwin and Heritage, 1990). Because of the influence of the early work in conversation analysis that looked only at mundane conversation (e.g., Sacks, Schegloff and Jefferson, 1974), mundane conversation has been awarded the status of privileged communication, so to speak. Goodwin and Heritage (1990) probably speak for the majority of conversation analysts when they say that mundane conversation is the "primordial site of language use," providing the "point of departure for more specialized communicative contexts . . . which may be analyzed as embodying systematic variations from conversational procedures." Robinson (1990) calls other communicative systems "dialects of mundane conversation." This assumption—that mundane conversation is the canonical form of communication, beside which all other forms are mere variants—concerns us here because it is clearly erroneous (as we argue below), and yet it has permeated much work on human-computer interaction (for example, Frolich and Luff, 1990; Norman and Thomas, 1990; Wooffitt, 1990; Allen, 1992).

Although most conversation analysts have studied mundane conversation and believe that it is "primordial," some researchers within the tradition of conversation analysis have cast a wider net, looking at a variety of communicative settings. Their work has convincingly demonstrated that conversation—and communication more generally—are fundamentally *practical* activities, geared and adapted to the particular circumstances of their use. Button (1990) has pointed out that many human-computer interaction researchers have missed this point entirely, and they inappropriately attempt to apply findings from analyses of *mundane conversation* to human-computer interaction design. But studies such as Atkinson (1982; 1990), Holstein (1988), Hutchins (1990a), and many papers in Tracy (1991) show that conversational formats and events vary by setting; that is, for a given conversational setting, the goals of participants and the constraints and opportunities afforded by the setting determine how the communication unfolds. To design a system of human-computer communication, it is imperative to understand the specific nature of the communicative setting. To blindly use mundane conversation as a model for human-computer communication is to miss the point that people tailor their communicative activities to the particularities of the situation, and that mundane conversation is but one model among many used by ordinary people in everyday life.

Because the assumption that conversation is the correct model for human-computer interaction is so pervasive and persistent, and because it is so important to look at the particularities of the communicative setting in order to understand how communication works, let's look in some detail at two studies (Atkinson, 1982; Holstein, 1988) that demonstrate that communication can only be analyzed and understood as a function of the goals of participants and of the constraints and opportunities of the communicative setting.

Atkinson (1982) studied language use in an English court and found that courtroom communication is much more formal and structured than mundane conversation. The general feel of a mundane conversation is free flowing and informal: features of mundane conversation such as turn-taking, repair, and conventions for opening and closing a conversation typically involve a great deal of negotiation among participants, and there is considerable latitude for what will happen next in the conversation (Atkinson, 1982; 1990; Goodwin and Heritage, 1990; Wooffitt, 1990). Atkinson found that, by contrast, in the English courtroom, patterns of conversation diverge markedly from those of mundane conversation. For example, the kind of turn taking characteristic of mundane conversation is absent. Participants do not negotiate turns as they do in conversation; rather, turns are "pre-allocated" such that counsel, witness, judge, defendant, arbitrator, and plaintiff all have slots during which they are allowed to be heard on specific subjects. For example, the first counsel may pose a question to a witness, at which time the second counsel may remonstrate, "Objection!" The second counsel may not, however, take this opportunity to communicate on some other matter, such as posing her own question to the witness, or requesting to hear from another witness, or asking when lunch will be. Nor should the witness answer the question until the judge has decided whether to sustain the objection. Atkinson (1982) provided a verbatim transcript of a segment of a trial during which a witness who did not understand the rules of the courtroom answered a question after an objection, before the judge's decision. The witness was admonished by the judge: "... when you hear the district attorney object, don't make any answer until I tell you you've to answer the question or not." Thus are the communicative rules of the courtroom learned and enforced. This degree of control over a conversational turn by a participant in a mundane conversation would be unimaginable.[3]

In an ethnographic study of involuntary commitment hearings of mental patients in California, Holstein (1988) showed that conversational events, at a very fine-grained level, are determined by the goals of conversational participants and by the opportunities and constraints of the conversational setting. Holstein found that the types of questions, the length of pauses, the extent to which patients were interrupted during testimony, and whether conversational indications of interest ("Really?", "Uh huh") were used depended on whether the patient was being questioned by a public defender or a district attorney. The goals of public defenders and district attorneys are diametrically opposed: a public defender wants to help the patient avoid involuntary hospitalization, while a district attorney seeks commitment of the patient. The goals of public defender and district attorney are the first primary determinants of the course of the conversation (as we shall see in more detail).

A second determinant of the course of the conversation concerns the opportunities and constraints of the particular courtroom setting in which the hearings are held. In the commitment hearings, both the public defender and the district attorney are in a conversational setting prone to an interesting possibility: the mental patient being evaluated for commitment may at any moment begin to "talk crazy." For public defenders, the possibility of "crazy talk" is a constraint; for district attorneys, it is an opportunity. Public defenders want to manage the conversation to prevent or shortcircuit delusional talk, while district attorneys want precisely the opposite—to get the patients to, as the district attorneys say, "hang themselves" through their "crazy talk." It is important to recognize that the determining influence on speech here is directly produced by the specific (opposing) *goals* of the public defender and the district attorney. The conversation is not determined by a mutually constructed context in which creating shared understanding is paramount, or by some general laws of conversation; it is directly determined by participants' goals. More specifically, it is determined by the goals of the powerful participants in the conversation; the patient is primarily responsive.[4]

The deliberate, goal-determined management of the conversational flow effected by public defenders and district attorneys is illustrated in the verbatim segments of hearing transcripts provided by Holstein (1988). In the first example, we find the public defender trying to minimize the impact of a patient's "crazy" talk.[5] Fred Smitz is being questioned by the public defender. The double slashes (//) indicate simultaneous speech:

Public Defender: Where would you live?

Fred Smitz: I think I'd go to a new board and care home not populated by rapists // and Iranian agents.

Public Defender: (breaking in) Fine, Mr. Smitz. Now would you take your medication?

Fred Smitz: I would if it didn't pass // through the hands of too many Russians.

Public Defender: (breaking in) Do you still get an SSI check, Mr. Smitz?

The public defender attempts to minimize the patient's delusional speech by breaking in when the patient begins to elaborate his answers to the questions. The public defender keeps the conversation rolling along, asking very directed questions with yes-no answers, trying to get the patient to give short, correct answers to the questions about medication, and so forth. He ignores the content of the delusional speech, behaving as though it did not occur.

By comparison, in a transcript with another patient, we find the district attorney doing exactly what the public defender was avoiding – encouraging the patient to elaborate delusional comments. This somewhat lengthy segment is given here just as Holstein (1988) reported it, to underscore the deliberate, persistent conversational tactics used by the district attorney to elicit the patient's "crazy talk." Note the district attorney's liberal use of silences and indications of interest, the absence of interruption, and the use of very open-ended questions—just exactly what the public defender was not doing. The district attorney is questioning Lisa Sellers:

District Attorney: How do you like your summer out here, Lisa?

Lisa Sellers: It's OK.

District Attorney: How long have you lived here?

Lisa Sellers: Since I moved from Houston.
(Silence.)

Lisa Sellers: About three years ago.

District Attorney: Tell me about why you came here.

Lisa Sellers: I just came.
(Silence.)
Lisa Sellers: You know, I wanted to see the stars, Hollywood.
(Silence.)
District Attorney: Uh huh.
Lisa Sellers: I didn't have no money.
(Silence.)
Lisa Sellers: I'd like to get a good place to live.
(Long silence.)
District Attorney: Go on. (spoken simultaneously with onset of next utterance)
Lisa Sellers: There was some nice things I brought.
(Silence.)
District Attorney: Uh huh.
Lisa Sellers: Brought them from the rocketship.
District Attorney: Oh really?
Lisa Sellers: They was just some things I had.
District Attorney: From the rocketship?
Lisa Sellers: Right.
District Attorney: Were you on it?
Lisa Sellers: Yeah.
District Attorney: Tell me about the rocketship, Lisa.

Holstein (1988) reported that on occasion a public defender believes that hospitalization is the best choice for a patient. When this happens, the conversation of the public defender takes on a distinctively district attorney-like flavor; as Holstein says, now "inappropriate talk [is] allowed to flourish."

The striking degree to which the goal-directed nature of communication is revealed in the English courtroom and the involuntary commitment hearings suggests that the first thing we must attend to in any attempt to design a system of communication is to assess goals, rather than to pay attention to such features as turn-taking and repair (as do Frolich and Luff, 1990; Norman and Thomas, 1990; Wooffitt, 1990; Allen, 1992, for example), which are situationally specific aspects of a particular conversational setting, not the general features of communication they have been assumed to be.

The studies by Atkinson (1982, 1990) and Holstein (1988) show that the notion that mundane conversation is "primordial" misses the point that human communication is, first and foremost, fundamentally *practical*. It varies, as we have seen, by setting and function.[6]

Wynn (1980) made the interesting point that the ambiguity and imprecision in mundane conversation itself may, in many situations, be functional and intentional; as she said, "The messiness, potential ambiguity, implicitness . . . of natural conversation serve many of the purposes that actors have, including [those of] intimacy and mutuality, [through means of] less and less explicit surface discourse." Even the very ambiguity of conversation, generally thought to be a problem to be remedied, may then, in some situations, serve a definite conversational purpose. Thus we must look to the *purposes* of communication to understand its shape and form.

There are many distinctive forms of human communication, each using language in its own way, for its own purposes. The way language is used in a ritual or a lecture, or a debate, or a courtroom summary, or a computer program is no more or less humanly possible or important than everyday conversation. Nor do these communicative settings constitute mere variants of mundane conversation; they embody their own intentions and conventions, carefully matched to the goals for which they will be used. Atkinson (1982) noted that many settings such as church services, conferences, meetings, and parliamentary proceedings have little in common with mundane conversation but share with each other characteristics of systematic, more formalized communication. Generally speaking, all cultures have a variety of ways of structuring language and controlling its use, and the problem, in any given instance, is to select or fashion an appropriate form, given the constraints and opportunities of the situation.

Robinson (1990), who is generally sanguine about the possibilities of applying conversation models to human-computer interaction, has nevertheless noted that, ". . . there is no guarantee that features found in mundane conversation, engineered into a human-computer interaction, will necessarily result in the same managed accomplishment observed in their original context." Indeed, as we have discussed, the importance of constructing a conversational context from prior knowledge and perceptual input suggests that such managed accomplishment is most unlikely, given the computer's limitations. For purposes of human-computer communication, we should not promote one style of communication over another until we have carefully considered the situation in which people and computers attempt to communicate. We should be particularly careful not to promote a style of communication based on prejudicial treatment of the computer, whose conversational resources are decidedly lacking, as Suchman (1987) and Winograd and Flores (1986) have shown. Instead, we should ask what it is we want to do with computers, examine the way in which resources are allocated among the parties to the communication, and then determine, based on this assessment of opportunities and constraints, how we can best communicate in the unique situation in which human and machine come together.

Though we may relinquish the conversational model with some regret, when we seek another model of human-computer interaction, we have the possibility to free ourselves of the serious liabilities of conversation. Conversation is characterized by ambiguity, lack of precision, and, sometimes, complete failure. These liabilities are particularly fatal for human-computer communication, though much less so for human-human communication.

In human conversations, people have developed repair mechanisms to mitigate ambiguity, imprecision, and failure (see Goodwin and Heritage, 1990; Wooffitt, 1990). But repair works imperfectly; as Schutz (1962) noted, in conversation, understanding is "without guarantees." For many conversational situations imperfect communication is acceptable; unambiguous, precise communication is not needed. Even when we completely fail to communicate with people, we often have the option of simply not speaking to them at all in the future. However, for communicating with a *machine*, we do not want to fail, and we want the ability to make unambiguous, precise statements so that the machine will do what we intend it to do. Thus it is not surprising that computer scientists have relied, from the outset, not on conversational communication but on formal languages for communicating with computers.

Formal languages are specifically designed to enable the kind of unambiguous, precise communication demanded by a machine. In conversational communication, the possibilities for interpretation introduced by context are virtually limitless; there is the potential for an infinite regress of interpretation because the knowledge that informs an interpretation can itself be questioned and must be explained by reference to other knowledge, which can itself be questioned and explained by still other knowledge, and so on, *ad infinitum* (Wynn, 1980; Suchman, 1987). It is precisely this element of interpretation that we must eliminate to communicate effectively with machines.

Mathematicians, logicians, philosophers, professional computer programmers, and other such folk routinely develop and use formal languages. But people not trained in these traditions often find their languages mystifyingly opaque, dense, and impenetrable. Within the world of computing, many people have had so much trouble with conventional programming languages that, as we have seen, there have been many calls to enable the computer to communicate the way people routinely do—through the "effortless" medium of conversation. However, if we look more closely, we observe that end users have had problems, not with programming languages *per se*, but with *specific* computer programming languages, namely, general languages such as C, Fortran, Lisp. But because of the difficulties end users have often had in learning these languages (Lewis and Olson, 1987; Soloway and Spohrer, 1989), alternatives to formal languages—especially natural language conversations—have been studied as potential replacements. We want to argue here that just as formal languages have served computer scientists well, they will serve end users well. There is nothing unnatural or peculiar in any way about formal communication. In the next chapter, we look at some different forms of formal communication that occur in everyday life to see that formal communication is natural and unproblematic for ordinary people. Once we see that, it frees us to imagine and design ways of communicating with computers that do not assume the priority of any single communicative convention; rather, we can direct our energies toward understanding the particular practical realities of the communicative situation of interest.

Unlike conversational communication, formal languages can be text-based or graphical. For many problems, a graphical representation is much the most "natural" (see Rich, 1985). Conversational communication can be quite constricting and unnatural when what is needed is fundamentally graphic. Again, the problem is one of matching the practical problem at hand to the design of the technology, rather than assuming *a priori* the primacy of one form of communication, i.e. conversation. In chapter 5 we explore visual application frameworks and their utility for end user systems.

SUMMARY

As noted earlier, Suchman (1987) and Winograd and Flores (1986) provide a detailed discussion of why computers cannot converse, and we have briefly recapped these arguments. We have argued that the computer's conversational disability needn't occasion dismay as far as human-computer communication goes. What has been taken as paradigmatic "conversation" really isn't paradigmatic (Atkinson, 1982; 1990; Holstein, 1988; Hutchins, 1990a; Tracy, 1991); people have many effective ways of communicating that do not involve conversation. The persistence of the conversational standard is, however, troubling. Suchman adopts a somewhat "no-exit" stance to her own critique; computers cannot converse, yet they must be held to the standard of conversation. As she says, "A growing corpus of observations from the analysis of everyday human conversation provides a baseline from which to assess the state of interactivity between people and machines." Since Suchman's analysis makes plain that machines cannot share in the resources people bring to conversation, and conversation is to be the "baseline from which to assess the state of interactivity between people and machines" where does that leave us? I think it would leave us rather high and dry if we were to continue to hold computers—or ourselves in all situations—to conversational standards. Communication is effected in many different ways, conversation being but one. It is time for us to let go of conversation as the "paradigm case" of human-computer interaction and look to the many practical means of communicating that people have invented. That is what we shall do in the next chapter.

3

Task-specific Programming Languages

By relieving the brain of all unnecessary work, a good notation sets it free to concentrate on more advanced problems.
—A. Whitehead, *An Introduction to Mathematics*

FORMAL SYSTEMS: SOME BACKGROUND

In 1979, as part of my anthropological training, I spent several months living in a primitive village perched atop a ridge in the mountains off the north coast of Papua New Guinea. Other villages on other ridgetops, and villagers out in their gardens miles away, were brought within range of village communication through a system of signals drummed out on slit-gongs—large wooden drums made of hollowed out tree trunks (see figure 3.1). A sophisticated language of signals allowed a wide variety of messages to be sent—to call a particular person in from his garden, to give notice of a meeting of villages for a specified day, to broadcast the sad news of the death of a relative.

Communication by slit-gong is nothing more or less than the invocation of a formal language, and it does not require any special abilities on the part of New Guineans to communicate in this fashion. A great many human communicative systems are formally structured in just this way. Within the study of human-computer interaction, this observation on the ordinariness of formal communication would be unremarkable were it not for a very strong current of thought that holds that end users should be shielded from having to use such formal languages; they should instead be provisioned with, for example, "conversational" user interfaces that promote informal discourse between human and computer (e.g., Frolich and Luff, 1990; Norman and Thomas, 1990;

Figure 3.1
A *garamut* or slit-gong from Madang Province, Papua, New Guinea. Photograph courtesy of Chris Darrouzet.

Wooffitt, 1990; Allen, 1992), or systems that enable programming via the specification of concrete examples (e.g. Maulsby, Witten and Kittlitz, 1989; Cypher, 1991; Myers, 1991). Before making specific proposals for the design of end user programming languages, we offer some simple observations about the ubiquity of formal languages in human life to argue that the avoidance of formal languages for end users is not necessary, and that the real question is how to design those languages. We consider a number of ordinary, non-computer-based systems that rely on formal communication to convince ourselves that for end users, formal languages are a perfectly suitable means of communication.

Many human activities, such as conducting a symphony, or indicating to a driver that it is her turn to stop at an intersection, or signaling to the pitcher to throw an inside curveball, are carried on via formal systems of communication. In everyday life, people learn and use a wide variety of formal languages and systems. These systems are so pervasive that we scarcely stop to notice them: the alphabet, numerals, games, methods for scoring games, arithmetic, algebra, shorthand, the conventions used in sewing, knitting and crochet patterns, copyediting marks, calendars, maps, money, musical notation, street and highway traffic control signs, and even the juvenile secret language "Pig Latin."[1] People have considerable facility with these systems; they learn to do arithmetic in more than one base, to work with different systems of numerals, to write in more than one style of the alphabet, to transpose music from one key to another. The pervasiveness of formal systems shows that people readily invent, learn, and use them. In the early part of the nineteenth century, as Charles Babbage set about to design his "Analytical Engine," people were already communicating with machines via formal machine languages. Babbage's design borrowed from one such language, that used to program power-driven looms. Babbage himself never actually built the Analytical Engine, but its computations were to be determined by a set of instructions delivered via punched cards, just like the punched cards that encoded woven fabric patterns for the intricately patterned jacquard cloth manufactured on the looms (Stein, 1985).

Formal systems are so pervasive because they are so useful; they allow effective communication in the many everyday situations in which explicitness and precision are needed to enable the practical fulfillment of goals. Controlling traffic, or explaining how a dress can be constructed, or deciding how much money is owed when all appropriate taxes have been added in are activities that are greatly facilitated by a system that precisely defines a set of elements and relations. Formal systems permit activity to unfold in such a way that tasks can be accomplished accurately and reliably. These examples of varied communicative forms are intended to suggest that, with respect to computers, our focus should be on the *accomplishment of tasks* and the formal communicative systems that best describe and support a set of tasks.

Perhaps it should not be surprising that people are adept at learning and using formal systems when we consider that the most fundamental form of human social organization in virtually every society is based on formal kinship systems. Each society has a way of unambiguously defining kin relations, and every member of the society learns these relations. This is not to say that people always adhere exactly to the rules set out by a kinship system (because individuals to fill appropriate roles such as eligible marriage partner may not be available at a given time), but every member of the society learns and understands what the system is and can reliably answer questions about the nature of the relations in the system.[2]

The ubiquity of kinship systems speaks to their utility; and perhaps the development of our ability to "define kin" which probably emerged many hundreds of thousands of years ago, was the beginning of our cognitive abilities to learn and use formal systems (see Wallace, 1961).

Formal Notations

So far we have avoided mention of notation; we have been exploring the ease with which people learn and use formal languages and the circumstances under which people find them useful. Some formal systems, such as kinship systems or slit-gong signals, do not even have a notation. Knowledge of kin relations is transmitted verbally and aural slit-gong signals have no written encoding.[3] However, notations do greatly facilitate the use of formal languages, and certainly they are an issue for any discussion of programming languages. Our argument is that not only do people readily learn and use formal languages, but they also readily learn the notations that go along with them.

There are many formal notations that are learned in the course of ordinary life: musical notation, arithmetic, algebra, the alphabet, conventions for copyediting, to name but a few. These notations are, in general, easily learned and readily applied. Learning them enables us to reproduce the tasks or events they describe accurately and reliably. The use of the notations requires no special abilities (given basic literacy), and yet they give us access to a rich store of encoded knowledge for an immensely varied set of tasks and events. As the great Russian psychologist Leont'ev (1974) remarked, "[Artifacts] mediate activity that connects a person not only with the world of objects, but also with other people. This means that a person's activity assimilates the experience of humanity."

We can also use notations to encode creations or observations of our own, preserving, for ourselves and others, the flow of a patterned activity. Some notations that describe ordinary activities actually look very much like conventional programming languages. We examine in some detail two such notations: baseball scoring notation and knitting instructions.

A baseball scoresheet (figure 3.2) is an ingenious form that permits a scorer to encode almost every event of a game for a given team on a single sheet of paper, providing the data to generate the relevant baseball statistics for the game and the players.[4] A standard set of symbols encode events of the game. For example, "HR" stands for home run, "2B" for

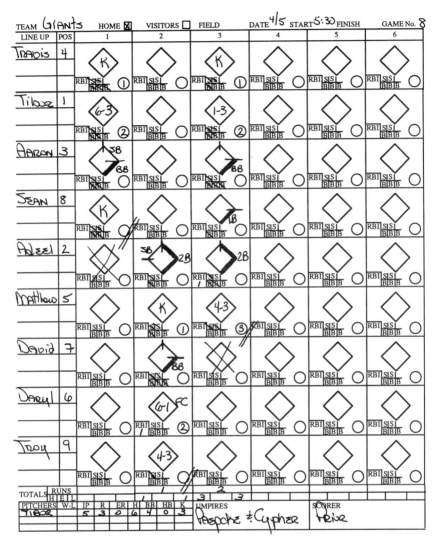

Figure 3.2
A baseball scoresheet. This is the official Little League baseball scoresheet. It has been filled out to show the events of a game.

double, "SB" for stolen base, "K" for strikeout, and so forth. There are fifteen such alphabetic symbols that describe batting events. (See figure 3.3.)[5] Seven symbols encode field events ("ETH-" for throwing error, "U" for unassisted play, "DP" for double play, etc.). Numerals 1-9 describe the field positions (1 for pitcher, 2 for catcher, 3 for first base, etc.). To

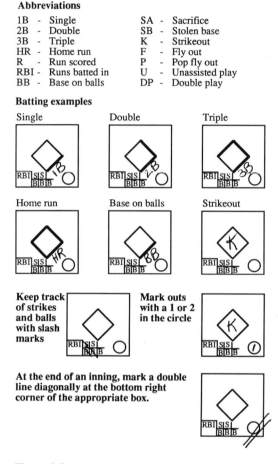

Abbreviations

1B	-	Single	SA	-	Sacrifice
2B	-	Double	SB	-	Stolen base
3B	-	Triple	K	-	Strikeout
HR	-	Home run	F	-	Fly out
R	-	Run scored	P	-	Pop fly out
RBI	-	Runs batted in	U	-	Unassisted play
BB	-	Base on balls	DP	-	Double play

Batting examples

Single   Double   Triple

Home run   Base on balls   Strikeout

Keep track of strikes and balls with slash marks

Mark outs with a 1 or 2 in the circle

At the end of an inning, mark a double line diagonally at the bottom right corner of the appropriate box.

Figure 3.3
Scorekeeper's Helper. This form enumerates the objects and actions of a game to remind scorers of the appropriate symbols to use.

record outs, the numbers of the fielders involved in the play to make the out are combined with the type of ball hit; for example, a man on first double play where the batter hits a ground ball to the third baseman is encoded "DP, 5-4-3." A fly ball to left field is recorded as "F-7."

In addition to the alphanumeric code, the baseball scoresheet also has a a graphic for organizing computation. The scoresheet's overall design is a table with cells for each "at-bat" event. A series of marks encode various events. Strikes and balls are recorded by making a mark through an "S" or a "B" in a small grid within an at-bat cell (see figure 3.2). Lines traced

Field positions

1 Pitcher	6 Shortstop
2 Catcher	7 Left field
3 First base	8 Center field
4 Second base	9 Right field
5 Thirdbase	

Infield scoring examples

To record an out, write the number of the defensive player who fields the ball, then the number of the player making the put-out.

Ground ball to the infield	Double play, runner on first

Ground out to third base

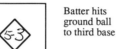

Batter hits ground ball to third base

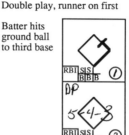

Ground out to shortstop

First base makes play unassisted

Batter hits ground ball to shortstop to end the inning

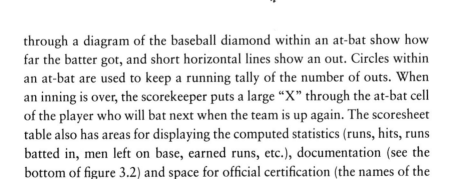

through a diagram of the baseball diamond within an at-bat show how far the batter got, and short horizontal lines show an out. Circles within an at-bat are used to keep a running tally of the number of outs. When an inning is over, the scorekeeper puts a large "X" through the at-bat cell of the player who will bat next when the team is up again. The scoresheet table also has areas for displaying the computed statistics (runs, hits, runs batted in, men left on base, earned runs, etc.), documentation (see the bottom of figure 3.2) and space for official certification (the names of the umpires and scorer, date, time, etc.).

That the baseball scoresheet notation is easily learned by ordinary people is evident from its use all over the United States by parents of Little Leaguers who are drafted to score their children's games. At Major League baseball games, many fans bring scoresheets with them and score the game as it proceeds, strictly for fun. The baseball scoresheet is something very like a paper form of a user programming system: a set of data (the events of the game encoded on the paper form) can be processed by applying the relevant formulas (such as computing averages, or adding up runs) to make the appropriate calculations. The human has to stand in as processor to perform the calculations, but the scoresheet provides the means by which the data are input, organized for processing, and then output as calculations displayed on the scoresheet.

Knitting patterns look remarkably like computer programs. Providing a description of how to knit a garment or household article involves the use of constructs familiar to programmers: modules of instructions, subroutines, global variables, means for specifying conditions, and iteration. For example, the following is a module of the instructions for knitting the "Anchors Aweigh Aran Afghan" (Cozy Afghans, 1989).[6]

DRUNKEN SAILOR CABLE
Worked on 12 sts.
NOTES: Front Cross (FC): Slip 2 sts to cable st holder and hold in front, k2, then k2 from holder. Back Cross (BC): Slip 2 sts to cable st holder and hold in back, k2, then k2 from holder. Increase (inc): Purl into front and back of same st.
ROW 1: (right side) P6, k4, p2.
ROWS 2, 4 and 6: K2, p4, k6.
ROW 3: P6, FC, p2.
ROW 5: P4, p2 tog, k4, inc. p1.
ROW 7: P5, FC, p3.
ROW 8 and all subsequent wrong side rows: Knit all knit sts and purl sts.
ROW 9: P3, p2 tog, k4, inc, p3.
ROW 11: P4, FC, p4.
ROW 13: P2, p2 tog, k4, inc, p3.
ROW 15: P3, FC, p5.
ROW 17: P1, p2 tog, k4, inc, p4.
ROW 19: P2, FC, p6.
ROW 21: P2, k4, p6.
ROW 23: P2, BC, p6.
ROW 25: P1, inc, k4, p2 tog, p4.
ROW 27: P3, BC, p5.

ROW 29: P2, inc, k4, p2 tog, p3.
ROW 31: P4, BC, p4.
ROW 33: P3, inc, k4, p2 tog, p2.
ROW 35: P5, BC, p3.
ROW 37: P4, inc, k4, p2 tog. p1.
ROW 39: P6, BC, p2.
ROW 40: K2, p4, k6. Repeat rows 1 through 40 for pattern.

This module of the pattern defines a program for executing the Drunken Sailor Cable that includes: defining subroutines for Front Cross (FC) and Back Cross (BC); specifying the condition under which the instructions at ROW 8 are executed (when the row is a wrong side row); and specifying the number of iterations needed to complete the module. The pattern contains nine other modules ("Anchor Stitch," "Little Waves Pattern," etc.) to make the complete afghan.

In addition to the instructions contained within each module, the pattern also establishes "global variables" for the gauge of the stitches:

GAUGE: 4 sts = 1 inch over stockinette st and garter st.
32 sts of Anchor Stitch = 8 inches.
19 sts of Little Waves Stitch = 4 inches.
12 sts of Drunken Sailor Cable = 2 inches.
10 sts of Cable = 2 inches.

The knitting instructions have several important similarities to the base-ball scoresheet: a great deal of information is contained within a terse set of instructions; the instructions (while appearing incomprehensible to non-knitters) are accessible to any ordinary person who decides to learn to knit; and, just as the filled-out scoresheet records the way a game unfolded, the knitting instructions provide a permanent record of the way the task of knitting an afghan unfolds, allowing an afghan of the same pattern to be produced by anyone anywhere, if the instructions are followed correctly.

End User Programming Should Be Fun
In addition to being useful, formal systems have an appeal all their own; people naturally gravitate to them. Games are perhaps the clearest example of the way we spontaneously engage in interaction with formal systems.[7]

There is generally no utilitarian value in a game (though some do manage to earn their living by leveraging the love of formal pursuits their less-skilled fellow humans indulge), yet we happily spend hours playing games and often learn extremely complex rules so that we can play them better.

Part of the attraction of game playing is the pleasure of mastering a difficult skill. But there is also a satisfaction in knowing and playing by the rules. This is most evident when watching, rather than playing, games, because now skill mastery is irrelevant. In spectator sports, or games such as chess, for example, audience participation in the game lies in the enjoyment derived from understanding how the game is played and in seeing the way the players take action within the strict limits of the rules of the game.[8]

An example of the sheer entertainment value of simply knowing the rules is illustrated by a commercial sponsored by IBM during televised sportscasts in which viewers are invited to play a game-about-the-game called "You Make the Call." The commercial shows a clip from a former game of a play that involves a tricky judgment, (e.g., under the circumstances, was the ball in play?, did the runner score?) and the viewer is asked to "make the call." To "win" you must have knowledge of esoteric rules of the game to determine how the call should have been made. The commercial opens with the posing of the question, then switches to the real commercial advertising IBM products, then returns to give the answer revealing the correct call. For many people, this kind of problem solving—which demands knowledge of a set of formal elements and rules about their relations—is a relaxing leisure time pursuit, a kind of "formality for fun." In questions involving games there is, very satisfyingly, an unambiguously right answer.

End user programming can be fun too. In the spreadsheet study, one of the pleasures of having done the research was to frequently hear people who have never taken a computer science class describe their work with spreadsheets as "fun." A cynic with tongue-in-cheek remarked to me that perhaps this is the most fun accountants can have, but it is safe to say that most designers would be happy to have millions of satisfied users enthusiastically and productively using their product.

We have considered some formal languages that are routinely used by ordinary people in everyday life. Some of the notations that encode these languages have much in common with computer languages, and yet they are indisputably used by people one would not ordinarily consider "technical." These examples show that ordinary people unproblematically learn and use formal languages and notations in everyday life. Now we must ask how this insight can be applied to the design of end user computing languages. In particular, we must ask what it is about these languages and notations that makes them so accessible.

FORMAL LANGUAGES FOR END USERS

To be application developers, end users need programming languages, just as professional programmers do. But the use of formal computing languages has been restricted, for the most part, to those willing to devote considerable time and energy to their study. We have argued that people are adept at learning formal systems and notations. If that is true, why then, have so many people had so much trouble learning conventional programming languages? The answer is that it is only when people have *a particular interest in something*, such as knitting or baseball, or producing budgets or designing printers, or simulating the behavior of clown fish or honeybees, that they readily learn the formal languages and notations that describe the elements and relations of the system of interest. It is the infusion of *interest* that enables a housewife who failed high school math to take a sewing pattern, alter it (which involves going from 2-space to 3-space and understanding the conventions of the sewing pattern to make the correct adjustments), and create a perfect garment. Taking an interest means that an otherwise arithmetically disinterested baseball fan can understand how to compute RBIs, ERAs,[9] batting averages, and a whole host of other baseball statistics, and he can remember, to a detailed level, the statistics associated with different players spanning many years. For the sports fan, these activities do not depend simply on knowing elementary arithmetic, though that is involved, but rather on understanding the formal semantics of what constitutes an RBI or an ERA (or whatever statistic) and taking a hearty interest in doing so.

People are likely to be better at learning and using computer languages that closely match their interests and their domain knowledge. This should not be surprising; an important thread of work in cognitive psychology has demonstrated that people perform better at cognitive tasks when the content of the problem is in a familiar domain (Price-Williams, 1962; Wason, 1966; Johnson-Laird and Wason, 1970; Wason and Johnson-Laird, 1972; Cole and Scribner, 1974; D'Andrade, 1989). For example, Price-Williams (1962) conducted a series of experiments with children in Nigeria to determine the effect of familiar materials on the task of classification. The children were able to successfully classify plants and animals—with which they were very familiar from their everyday experience—into appropriate groupings. However, they did poorly on classification tasks involving pictures of triangles, circles, and other idealized geometric forms with which they were unfamiliar. Wason and Johnson-Laird performed a series of experiments in which people were given reasoning problems that were logically equivalent, but differed in content (Wason, 1966; Johnson-Laird and Wason, 1970; Wason and Johnson-Laird, 1972). People consistently performed better at problems couched in familiar terms; for example, people were able to solve a logic problem involving cars and trains much more readily than a more abstract number-letter version of the same problem. (Johnson-Laird, [1983] went on to create a controversial explanation for these results involving people's putative use of "mental models," but whether we accept the notion of mental models or not, the experimental results are interesting and useful in themselves.) D'Andrade (1989) summarizes other such experimental findings. Gardner (1985) nicely pulls out the main contribution of this line of research:

The soundness, the speed, and the complexity of the reasoning that individuals exhibit seem primarily a function of the degree of familiarity and organization of the materials being processed, rather than a function of any special or general ability of the person doing the reasoning. And so there are appreciable differences in how a given person can reason about different topics, topics that, from a formal point of view, call upon the same degree (and even principles) of logical expertise. (Gardner, 1985)

Thus it is not surprising that users who reject conventional programming languages—which do not draw upon a familiar well of domain knowledge or interest for most people—may do very well at learning spreadsheets, CAD systems, statistical packages, and other task-specific programs. A key to understanding end users' interactions with computers is to recognize that end users are not simply underskilled programmers who need assistance learning the complexities of programming. Rather, they are not programmers at all. They are business professionals or scientists or librarians or teachers or other kinds of domain specialists whose jobs involve computational tasks. As the introduction to *Advanced Techniques in AutoCAD* states, "This book assumes that you are a drawing professional, more interested in maximizing your use of AutoCAD than in becoming a professional computer programmer" (Thomas, 1988). The design of end user programming languages should take into account users' interests, knowledge, and motivation, and their relationship to the computer, which is generally task-oriented.

The conclusion to draw from our observation that people learn formal languages unproblematically in familiar domains, when they are properly interested and motivated, is that end user programming languages should be *task-specific*. Language primitives should map to tasks in the domain the user understands. Task-specificity has two advantages: (1) it affords users ready understanding of what the primitives of the language do (because they already know them from their task domain), and (2) it eases application development because users can directly express domain semantics in the high-level operations of the language—there is no need to string together lower-level operations to get the desired behavior.

When end users attempt to learn programming languages that are *not* task-specific and do not have familiar primitives, many have serious difficulties. Lewis and Olson (1987) studied the problems end users have with conventional programming languages, and they identified working with low-level programming primitives as one of the major barriers to programming. They reported that users have difficulties both in learning the unfamiliar primitives themselves and then in learning how to assemble the primitives into functioning programs. Programming with low-level primitives is difficult for end users because the primitives are unrelated to the tasks and concepts they understand ("char*" or "cons" are not exactly familiar concepts from the everyday life world). In addition, "It is hard to see what combination of primitives will produce the correct task-related behavior" (Lewis and Olson, 1987; see also Du Boulay, 1989; Spohrer and Soloway, 1989). Without the motivation of wanting to become professional computer programmers, many end users get discouraged at the amount of work necessary to master a conventional programming language, and they discontinue study. Others never even try to learn; they have heard enough from those who have tried to avoid the subject altogether.

Our basic argument is that the problem with programming is not programming; it is the languages in which people are asked to program. The difficulty for end users has been that, for the most part, we have not developed the *right* formal languages to meet their needs. In a few cases, when we have developed such languages, end users have been spectacularly successful in programming their own applications. The well-known success stories are spreadsheets (Kay, 1984; Hutchins, Hollan and Norman, 1986; Lewis and Olson, 1987; Arganbright, 1986; Nardi and Miller, 1990; 1991; Nardi and Zarmer, 1991), CAD systems (Petre and Green, 1991; Gantt and Nardi 1992; Tee, 1992), statistical packages, and programs such as Mathematica. Stephen Wolfram, the inventor of Mathematica, has remarked, "Mathematica's success is based on a trick. Introducing a new [programming] language doesn't work ... but people will embrace what looks like a useful new application in itself." The source of the success of the formal end user programming languages in these software systems is that the language primitives are the application-level primitives with which users are already familiar. A mathematician, in a broad sense, already knows Mathematica, an accountant already knows Lotus 1-2-3, a statistician already knows SPSS.

The idea of task-specific programming languages for end users is not new. In 1967, James Martin envisioned that users would have available many "problem-oriented" computer languages:

Much of the development in the years to come will probably be in the area of languages, especially languages for on-line use. Now [that] we have this immensely powerful tool available to us, it is important to extend its use to the maximum number of people. We must develop languages that the scientist, the architect, the teacher, and the layman can use without being computer experts. The language for each user must be as *natural* as possible to him. The statistician must talk to his terminal in the language of statistics. The civil engineer must use the language of civil engineering. When a man learns his profession he must learn the *problem-oriented languages* to go with that profession. (Martin, 1967) (emphasis in original)

The widespread use and success of spreadsheets, statistical packages, and CAD systems postdate Martin's statement of the idea of problem-oriented languages. They are a tribute to his prescience, and his understanding of the needs of end users. An important part of Martin's vision, however, has not yet been realized: the easy availability of end user programming systems for smaller niches of users whose computing needs are more specialized than, but just as important as those of systems that command large markets. Task-specific programming languages and environments that would allow users who do not belong to vast market segments to create their own applications have not yet been developed, except as expensive and relatively inflexible custom solutions to specific problems for specific users.

THE SPREADSHEET FORMULA LANGUAGE

The spreadsheet formula language is an example of the kind of task-specific end user programming language we are advocating.[10] It is expressive and easy to learn and use. We examine the formula language here as an exemplar for other task-specific programming languages that can be developed for users in other domains, with other tasks. To start, let's look briefly at the expressivity of spreadsheets.

Expressivity

Spreadsheet users create an impressive variety of surprisingly rich and sophisticated applications (Nardi and Miller, 1990; 1991). Spreadsheets allow users to program complex applications that establish many relations between entities within a large problem space. In the spreadsheet applications that we collected as part of our study, we found many complex models expressive of rich domain semantics. To provide an example of this complexity, we have annotated, with arrows, a typical spreadsheet application to show the dependencies among cell values that model the user's problem (figures 3.4 and 3.5). (This is an actual spreadsheet from our study; identifying details have been changed.) This spreadsheet is expressive of a great deal of rich domain knowledge, but its complexity lies in *the relationships between entities in the domain itself*—not in the programming needed to create the formulas that model the relationships. The relations modeled in this spreadsheet are expressed entirely within the formula language. It is possible to express rich relational semantics within a spreadsheet because the spreadsheet formula language provides *high-level, task-specific programming primitives*, *accessibility*, and *simple but useful control constructs*. We look at each of these key features of the spreadsheet formula language in turn.

BogusCo, International
Changes in Working Capital
FY 88

	Balance Sep-87	Difference	Balance Sep-88	Total Net Change	Translation
Short term investments	1,000	248	1,248	248	0
Receivables	85,626	2,786	88,412	2,446	340
Inventories	54,460	(4,862)	49,598	(5,343)	481
Prepaid Expenses	1,373	62	1,435	61	1
Deferred Income Taxes	1,949	3,932	5,881	3,932	0
Total Current Assets	144,408	2,166	146,574	1,344	822
Bank Notes Payable	(25,937)	1,779	(24,158)	1,869	(90)
Current Portion LTD	(1,838)	1,205	(633)	1,187	18
Trade Accounts Payable	(8,012)	432	(7,580)	413	19
Other Accrued Expense	(21,314)	(6,089)	(27,403)	(6,206)	117
Warranty Reserve	(6,941)	(157)	(7,098)	(133)	(24)
ROUNDING	(1)	1			1
Total Current Liabilities	(64,043)	(2,829)	(66,872)	(2,870)	41
TOTAL	80,365	(663)	79,702	(1,526)	863
Notes Payable		1,779		1,869	(90)
Long term Debt		1,205		1,187	18
Other WC		(3,647)		(4,582)	935
Total		(663)		(1,526)	863
Other WC		(3,647)		(4,582)	935
Minority interest		804		804	
Total Other WC		(2,843)		(3,778)	935
Other accrued expenses		-6,206			
Minority interest		804			
Net other accrued expenses		-5,402			

Figure 3.4
A typical spreadsheet application collected in the spreadsheet study. Identifying
details have been changed.

High-level, Task-specific Programming Primitives

The spreadsheet formula language allows users to compute values in their
models by expressing relations among cell values. To use the formula language, the user must master only two concepts: cells as variables and
functions as relations between variables. With relatively little study, the
user acquires the means to solve the basic computational problems of any

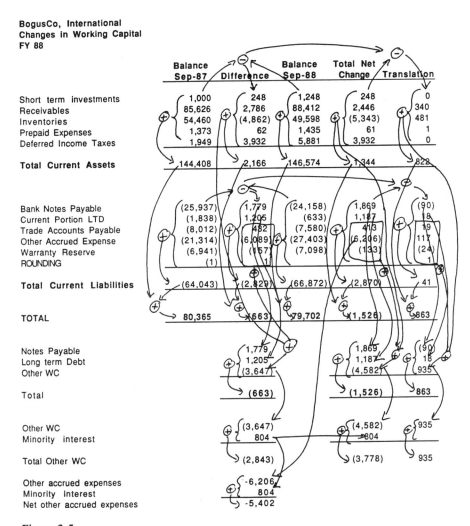

Figure 3.5
The same spreadsheet with annotations showing model relations

modeling task: creating entities that represent the variables in the problem and expressing relations among the entities. The formula language offers arithmetic, financial, statistical, and logical functions. Most spreadsheets also offer simple database functions, date and time functions, and error-trapping functions. In our study we found that most users normally use fewer than ten functions in their models; typically these include the basic arithmetic and rounding functions. (Imagine being restricted to ten functions in C or Lisp.) Even with such a small, easily learned number of operations, users can create the kind of complex spreadsheet of figure 6.

Spreadsheet users are productive with a small number of functions because the functions are high-level, task-specific operations that do not have to be built up from lower-level primitives. General programming languages are composed of a fairly large number of primitive functions and constructs because if you know how to combine them correctly, you can write an amazing variety of programs. The spreadsheet formula language, on the other hand, offers a smaller number of primitives that map directly onto operations that users within a specific range of applications need, such as taking averages, rounding numbers, and the basic arithmetic operations. For example, spreadsheet users do not have to know how to string together a series of functions to perform an operation such as "average," which is offered as a direct operation needing only its arguments. They do not have to declare data types; with so few primitives, only a few datatypes are possible. The formula language has much less flexibility and generality than a general programming language, but the learning curve is flatter, and *the basic operations accomplish tasks that users want to do.*

What this means is that task-specificity affords not only familiarity, with its associated benefits, but also simplicity and rapid development. The spreadsheet formula language is simple not just because everyone knows how to add and subtract and take averages (a statistical package might be just as simple for statisticians, but have primitives unfamiliar to most people), but because adding and subtracting and taking averages is what accountants, financial planners, and other kinds of spreadsheet users *do*. Their work is made simple by having the correct primitives ready-to-hand. There is no need to string together lower-level primitives; the primitives already do what needs to be done. There is also no need to allocate memory, make up variable names (cells are named by their position in the grid), include files, or do any number of tiresome programming chores necessary in other languages. For example, to sum eight values adjacent to one another in the spreadsheet table, the user writes: SUM(C1..C8). In a conventional language a special SUM operation would have to be created out of the addition operator to do this. Most likely, the user would also have to allocate memory, create variable names, declare datatypes, and so forth. The spreadsheet user has *direct access* to the primitives of the language and can write formulas without having to descend to a lower conceptual level at which issues relevant to the computer itself, but not the user, must be dealt with.

It is very important from a motivational standpoint that users attain early success with the system they are using (Warner, 1990; Nardi and Miller, 1991). It is not enough to say that users need systems that are "easy to use"; end user programming systems should allow users to solve simple problems within their domain of interest *within a few hours of use*.

Although it is possible to complete an instructional exercise in a general programming language after a few hours of work with the language, the student is a long way from the completion of a real application. Just the opposite is true with spreadsheets—after a small investment of time, the beginning spreadsheet user has a functioning program of real use, not just a toy program or completed exercise. The spreadsheet user's first efforts yield a complete application, rather than the partial solution that would result from trying to write the same application in a general programming language. Users do not have to learn every feature of a programming system in such a short time (in fact, as we will argue later, that would not be desirable), but they must be able to get some real work done and attain a sense of accomplishment and success. The "having to know everything to do anything" syndrome has stopped many a student of conventional languages, and it is a pitfall we should assiduously avoid in designing end user programming languages.

As users become more proficient at using spreadsheets, they learn more advanced programming concepts such as relative and absolute cell references, controlling the order of operations, and more sophisticated ways to copy, move and load data. Knowing the more advanced concepts is immensely useful, but we want to emphasize that *they are not necessary* for beginning users building simple spreadsheets. Spreadsheets allow users to perform useful work with a small investment of time and then to go on to more advanced levels of understanding as they are ready. In our research, we found that users often add new programming concepts to their repertoire very slowly, all the while being very productive spreadsheet users (Nardi and Miller, 1991).

Accessibility

The spreadsheet formula language is accessible because its task-specific operations are already familiar to users with applications requiring numeric manipulation. In addition, users can invoke the operations without having to do the tedious non-task/domain-related activities required in general programming languages such as declaring data types, including files, naming variables, "making" the system, and compiling. Being free of the tedium of low-level programming minutiae allows users to concentrate on the problem at hand, to be engaged with the problem-solving semantics of the application itself.

This kind of engagement, both in terms of having access to task-specific operations and freedom from low-level programming details, is true "direct manipulation" (see Shneiderman, 1983; Hutchins, Hollan, and Norman, 1986). It has nothing to do with input devices or user interface techniques; such engagement is much deeper, manifesting itself in the very foundations of the semantic design of the software system. The earliest spreadsheets (such as VisiCalc and early versions of Lotus 1-2-3) were ghastly by today's user interface design standards (obscure command names, completely text-based, etc.), but they were immediate successes with ordinary end users who recognized in them the high level of support for their own problem-solving tasks.

Control Constructs

Many empirical studies of novice programmers have found that beginning users often have great difficulty understanding control constructs in programming languages (Lewis and Olson, 1987; Hoc, 1989; Kahney, 1989; Kessler and Anderson, 1989; Spohrer, Soloway and Pope, 1989). Because program control is so central to accomplishing anything with a programming language, an immediate barrier has been thrown up, inhibiting the user's progress and creating a seriously demotivating force as the user tries to learn to program.

Spreadsheets eliminate this barrier by providing greatly simplified control constructs. Spreadsheets give users the power needed to write conditional statements, to iterate operations, and to maintain dependencies, but with little programming effort and with conceptual simplicity. The key to providing program control for end users seems to be keep control constructs simple (see Du Boulay, 1988, on simplicity).

A conditional in a spreadsheet formula might look like this:

IF(B12 > 100, B12, 100)

In this formula, if the value in cell B12 is greater than 100, then return the value of the cell, otherwise return the value 100. Conditionals can also be nested within formulas. Any formula, number, string, or cell reference can appear as a condition, and a result can be either a number or a string.

A conditional in a spreadsheet formula is easy to understand because it does not transfer control from one part of the spreadsheet to another. Its effects are local to the individual cell; the user can keep track of its effects because they do not ramify throughout the program. Thus a major source of potential complexity is avoided, while at the same time the user has the flexibility to set up local conditions.

In our study, users made frequent use of conditionals, including nested conditionals. "Jennifer," for example, a competent but not unusually sophisticated spreadsheet user, describes her formulas as "simple," even though she uses nested "ifs".

Interviewer: Okay, and the formulas that you have used, are they complicated or simple or both?

Jennifer: Ah, to me they are simple. I'm aware that there are other [functions] out there that I haven't used that I would like to learn to use, but usually, just, well, I use a lot of "if" statements. . . . And that's probably one of the most complex ones I do. I've had "if" statements that have had eight "ifs" in them.

Iteration in spreadsheets is also simple, especially in terms of programming mechanics. Users can select a range of cells over which to iterate an operation. (A range is a rectangular block of cells.) Returning to our summation example, SUM(C1..C8), the user writes a simple formula that specifies the sum operation and the cells that contain the values to be summed. The cell range is specified compactly by its first and last cell; for example, SUM(C1..C8) sums cells 1 to 8 in column C. The range could also be selected from the table itself with the mouse or cursor keys. In a conventional programming language, computing this sum would require at least writing a loop iterating through elements of an array, and establishing and naming a loop counter and summation variable. Spreadsheet functions obviate the need to create variable names and to create intermediate variables to hold results—non-task-related actions that many users find confusing and burdensome (Lewis and Olson, 1987). Instead, the user writes a simple formula that specifies the sum operation and the cells that contain the values to be summed.

Another form of iteration in spreadsheets is copying formulas (Sajaniemi and Pekkanen, 1988). When a formula is copied from one cell to another, its cell references are automatically changed so that the new formula's cell references are relative to the new cell (unless the user has specified an absolute cell reference).

Perhaps the most important source of control in spreadsheets is the managing of the dependencies between cell values. Users' formulas contain an implicit flow of control as any arbitrary cell can be related to any other. When a value in one cell changes, it may trigger a series of changes in dependent cells. This is the very basis of the spreadsheet's functionality, and it is quite powerful. Users can begin by building simple cell relations and move on to more elaborate models as their knowledge expands. In spreadsheets the mechanics of managing cell dependencies and their updates are completely taken care of by the spreadsheet itself—no programming effort at all is required on the part of the user. An important aspect of program control has been completely encapsulated by the spreadsheet, giving users the power of establishing and maintaining dependencies but requiring no low-level programming to accomplish these tasks. The user declares dependencies, and the spreadsheet provides the machinery to create them. Managing dependency relationships is a particularly good example of the way in which an end user programming system can allow users to focus on their domain-related problems at a very high level. Users need not go without sophisticated means of program control, but they themselves do not have to do the lower-level programming necessary to have them.

Spreadsheets, then, offer a set of very useful control structures—conditionals in formulas, iteration over cell ranges, and the modeling of cell dependencies through one-way constraints. But these control constructs are characterized by conceptual clarity and simplicity in terms of required programming effort. There is some programming to be done by the user, but much of the lower-level programming has been taken care of. The lesson to be drawn from spreadsheets is that control structures should be kept straightforward and simple. Where there is complexity, as in managing dependencies, the system should do as much as possible, leaving users only the task of understanding dependencies at a high semantic level. Spreadsheet control structures enable users to capture complex domain relationships expressed through conditions, iteration, and constraints, but at a low programming cost.

The Textual Nature of the Formula Language

Spreadsheets provide a visual programming framework that organizes computation, as we discuss at length in chapter 4. For the present, we want to point out that the formula language itself is entirely *textual*. Though several lines of research on end user programming proceed from the assumption that graphical techniques such as as visual programming (Chang, Ichikawa, and Ligomenides, 1986; Chang, 1990; Eisenstadt et al., 1990; Ladret and Rueher, 1991) and program induction (Maulsby, Witten, and Kittlitz, 1989; Myers, 1991) will provide significant leverage to end users, we question whether graphics per se is really the key to user programming languages. A limited language of high-level functions is more important than the particular form the language takes. The languages in statistical packages and programs such as Mathematica, as well as CAD macro languages and CAD extension languages such as AutoLISP, are purely textual. In the spreadsheet study, we asked users to discuss the disadvantages of spreadsheets. Not one user mentioned difficulties with the formula language (though users had other specific complaints about spreadsheets). Syntax is often suggested as a problem area in textual languages, but in our study users reported that syntax errors were few once they were familiar with a spreadsheet. Users noted that, in any case, most such errors are immediately caught by the spreadsheet itself, which will not permit poorly formed formulas. Proper syntax checking appears to be sufficient to enable users to cope with syntax errors. Textual languages are compact, efficient, and can be developed in less time than graphical languages. These are significant advantages that should be considered in the development of end user programming languages.

The combination of attributes in the spreadsheet formula language strikes a fine balance between expressivity and simplicity. The formula language provides a limited set of carefully chosen, high-level, task-specific operations that are sufficient for building applications within a restricted domain and a set of simple but useful control constructs. The operations and control constructs in spreadsheets are ready-to-hand; they do not require lower-level programming chores such as memory allocation, but are available at the highest level, so that users map them directly to their tasks. With spreadsheets, users have sufficient means to model their problems, but at a very attractive price in terms of programming effort.

The ability to create applications with only a few functions is an important benefit of spreadsheets that cannot be overemphasized. This pattern of the usage of a small number of constructs is not unique to spreadsheets: it has also been observed among CAD users (Tee, 1992) and UNIX users (Greenberg and Witten, 1988). Users have specific tasks to accomplish within their domain of interest. They want functionality that matches those tasks at a high level such that they do not have to either learn or use lower-level primitives. Task-specific functions allow users to develop quick facility with a program and to build a real application, however simple, in a short time. The motivational barrier is thus breached as users achieve rapid success. As users continue to use a program, they are not constantly faced with the job of stringing together lower-level functions as they work but can concentrate on the actual problem solving itself.

PROBLEMS OF TASK-SPECIFIC PROGRAMMING LANGUAGES

The task-specific language approach is not without its problems. First, it is expensive to build the many different task-specific languages that are needed for the myriad uses to which computers are put, or could be put. Further progress in reusable software components will be needed to alleviate this problem, to bring down the cost of developing task-specific systems. We discuss reuse more fully in chapter 7. A second possible problem with a plethora of task-specific programs is that users will be forced to switch between many different systems, learning a new user interface every time. The third, and most serious, problem is that it is difficult to know just how specific a task-specific system should be.

Switching between different programs implies that users will have to learn many different task-specific, and therefore non-standard user interfaces. But user interface consistency can be addressed at several levels. At the lowest level, it would be a good idea if every tool had a similar way of invoking common operations such as "quit." The label or command name for such operations should be the same for almost every application. At higher levels, closer to the application itself, matching tasks and domain semantics become more important than blind imposition of consistency rules (see Grudin, 1989). For example, outlines and slides are different; the manner of selecting a component in an outline might well be different from the manner of selecting a component in a slide.

In addition, we can expect to find some measure of user interface consistency within related applications. For example, all of the spreadsheet-based products—across many vendors and platforms—share a basic user interface. In particular, they share the tabular framework in which a spreadsheet user works, even when operation names, syntactical conventions, and other aspects of the user interface vary. There will also be consistency within related application families; that is, the specializations of extensible systems that evolve as users create and share applications within a single system such as FrameMaker,[11] or a CAD system. For example, FrameMaker users may create slide templates that provide functionality specific to slides. They don't have to learn a new program to make slides, they can use a program with which they are already familiar. When specializations grow out of a single basic system, the overhead costs are minimized because users are working within a known system. The notion of families of shared, specialized, task-specific applications holds much promise for providing both consistency and flexibility.

Still, there is the question: just how specific should a task-specific language be? Tee (1992) found an interesting pattern among users of mechanical engineering CAD systems: users created their designs out of only about five geometric features that were a mix of flexible, customizable features, such as protrusions, cuts, and patterns, and a few more specialized features such as tapers, flanges, ribs, and necks. All users used the flexible features while the choice of specialized features depended on the user's domain area. A flange, for example, can be created out of a cut and a protrusion, so users who only use flanges once in a while preferred to compose the flange out of the more general features. On the other hand, users who routinely created parts that are injection molded or cast chose to use tapers because they frequently needed them (Tee, 1992).

From a broad perspective, application constructs such as cuts and protrusions are clearly highly task-specific. Looking more closely within the domain of mechanical design, they can be seen to be less task-specific than flanges, tapers, and so forth. It seems that the only way to know how specific a set of program constructs should be is to study the domain very carefully to ascertain how tasks are broken down and performed. A guiding principle is that users will want to be able to create their applications with only a few basic operations, as the experience of UNIX users (Greenberg and Witten, 1988), spreadsheet users (Nardi and Miller, 1990) and CAD users (Tee, 1992) shows.

Another dimension to consider in the quest for task specificity is the extent to which the system is extensible. Do we want systems such as FrameMaker that specifically support text formatting and that can be specialized to support more specific applications, such as slide making, or do we want systems that specifically support slide making, such as PowerPoint?[12] The answer depends on the particular mix of applications that a user typically creates. If all a user ever does is create slides, and not too much flexibility is needed, then PowerPoint is a good choice. However, if a user does many kinds of text formatting chores and needs the flexibility of an extensible system, then a system such as FrameMaker is a better choice, all other things being equal. Of course, all other things may not be equal, and the ease of use of a system like PowerPoint may be attractive to many users who do not want the overhead of learning a system such as FrameMaker, even though they might sooner or later benefit from its flexibility. Ideally then, what we would like are systems that are (1) more task-specific than general programming languages, (2) extensible in the way that spreadsheets, FrameMaker, and other such systems are, and (3) easy to use.

The importance of ease of use in end user programming languages should not be underestimated. Systems such as HyperTalk[13] and GNU Emacs Lisp (Stallman, 1987) are extensible systems with some task-specific primitives, and yet neither has proven to be a successful end user language. GNU Emacs Lisp is fully extensible and contains task-specific primitives that give users high-level access to the task semantics of text editing and file management. However, programming in GNU Emacs Lisp has never penetrated to end users; it is used by professional programmers.[14] This is because, despite the task-specific primitives, to use GNU Emacs Lisp it is still necessary to learn the Lisp substrate in order to get at the task-specific primitives. Now we are back to all the old problems of learning and using general programming languages described by Lewis and Olson (1987), Soloway and Spohrer (1989), and others. A task-specific language such as the spreadsheet formula language succeeds where GNU Emacs Lisp fails because users can learn enough of the formula language in a few hours to create real applications. Learning enough Lisp to create GNU Emacs Lisp applications is a much more arduous and lengthy undertaking.

What about HyperCard? HyperCard with HyperTalk is a compromise between a general programming language and a task-specific language. HyperTalk doesn't do everything that a general programming language does, but it does provide a friendlier syntax than, say, C++. Like spreadsheets, it is interactive. But there is very little in the way of serious commercial stackware.[15] To create stackware or applications that are not simple prototypes, users are faced with learning HyperTalk, which is almost as complex as a conventional programming language and requires mastering basic computer science concepts. The problem may be that HyperCard-like environments are actually a bad compromise: they have the complexity of conventional programming languages but lack their speed and they are not close enough to end users' needs to provide the right kind of task specificity, nor are they general enough to be as powerful as a conventional language.

STUDYING TASKS

Deciding how task-specific a system should be, and deciding which operations constitute a fundamental layer and which an advanced layer, require a thorough understanding of users' tasks. The only way to acquire that understanding is to intensively study the tasks a system is intended to support. There are many approaches to such study, including traditional ethnography (Glaser and Strauss, 1967), situated action models (Lave, 1988), activity theory (Leont'ev, 1978), distributed cognition (Flor and Hutchins, 1991), and more narrowly focused methods such as GOMS modeling (Card, Moran and Newell, 1983). See Nardi (1992) for a comparison of situated action models, distributed cognition, and activity theory. Blomberg et al. (1992) provide a detailed description of the application of ethnographic methods to design problems, as well as a good bibliography. In assembling a design team, a person who is prepared to do an in-depth study of users' tasks, especially someone with training in the behavioral sciences, is invaluable.

Brooks (1991) argues that human-computer interaction studies will be most valuable to designers when they can provide (1) a broad background of comparative understanding over many domains, (2) high-level analyses useful for evaluating the impact of major design decisions, and (3) information that suggests actual designs, rather than simply general design guidelines or metrics for evaluation. To be able to provide such information, we must develop an appropriate analytical abstraction that "discards irrelevant details while *isolating and emphasizing those properties of artifacts and situations that are most significant for design*" (Brooks 1991) (emphasis added). Brooks (1991) has proposed the construction of a task taxonomy for comparative task analysis that would give researchers a framework in which to place tasks and would provide a good starting point from which to approach the design of a new system. It was not Brooks's intention to say just how to conduct the studies that will provide this information, but that question must be considered.

Two approaches that seem especially appropriate for studying technology are activity theory and distributed cognition. They are frameworks that will repay study for those interested in developing a principled means of performing task analyses. Activity theory and distributed cognition are briefly summarized here to give readers a sense of their conceptual richness. These approaches are useful in attempting to take into account both individual cognition and the social bases of cognitive activity. Thus they stand in contrast to traditional cognitive science, with its focus on mental representations inside a single person's head, and traditional anthropology and sociology where analysis begins at the sociocultural level with scant attention to individuals. Activity theory and distributed cognition are evolving approaches that have by no means solved all of the problems of studying tasks, or technology, or anything else, but they are sophisticated theoretical frameworks worthy of our attention.

Activity Theory

Work on activity theory began by the Russian psychologist Leont'ev in the former Soviet Union in the 1920's. Activity theory is complex and can only be partially sketched here, but see Leont'ev (1974), Bødker (1990), and Kuutti (1991) for summaries; and Leont'ev (1978), Wertsch (1981), Davydov, Zinchenko and Talyzina (1982), and Raeithel (1991) for more extensive treatment. This discussion focuses on a core set of concepts from activity theory that we believe is relevant for studies of technology.

In activity theory the unit of analysis is an activity. Leont'ev (1974) describes an activity as being composed of *subject, object, actions*, and *operations*. A subject is a person or a group engaged in an activity. An object (in the sense of "objective") is held by the subject and motivates activity, giving it a specific direction: "... behind the object there always stands a need or a desire, to which [the activity] always answers" (Leont'ev, 1974).

Actions are goal-directed processes that must be undertaken to fulfill the object. They are conscious (because one holds a goal in mind), and different actions may be undertaken to meet the same goal. For example:

> ... a person may have the object of obtaining food, but to do so he must carry out actions not immediately directed at obtaining food ... His goal may be to make a hunting weapon. Does he subsequently use the weapon he made, or does he pass it on to someone else and receive a portion of the total catch? In both cases, that which energizes his activity and that to which his action is directed do not coincide. (Leont'ev, 1974)

Actions are similar to what are often referred to in the human-computer interaction literature as *tasks* (e.g., Norman, 1991). Activities may overlap in that different subjects engaged together in a set of coordinated actions may have multiple or conflicting objects (Kuutti, 1991).

Actions also have operational aspects, that is, the way the action is actually carried out. Operations become routinized and unconscious with practice. When learning to drive a car, the shifting of the gears is an *action* with an explicit goal that must be consciously attended to. Later, shifting gears becomes operational and "can no longer be picked out as a special goal-directed process: its goal is not picked out and discerned by the driver; and for the driver, gear shifting psychologically ceases to exist" (Leont'ev, 1974). Operations depend on the conditions under which the action is being carried out. If a goal remains the same while the conditions under which it is to be carried out change, then "only the operational structure of the action will be changed" (Leont'ev, 1974).

Activity theory holds that the constituents of activity are not fixed but can change as conditions change. All levels can move both up and down (Leont'ev, 1974). As we saw with gear shifting, actions become operations as the driver habituates to them. An operation can become an action when "conditions impede an action's execution through previously formed operations" (Leont'ev, 1974). For example, if one's mail program ceases to work, one continues to send mail by substituting another mailer, but it is now necessary to pay conscious attention to using an unfamiliar set of commands. Notice that here the object remains fixed, but goals, actions, and operations change as conditions change. As Bødker (1989) points out, the flexibility recognized by activity theory is an important distinction between activity theory and other frameworks such as GOMS. Activity theory "does not predict or describe each step in the activity of the user (as opposed to the approach of Card, Moran and Newell, 1983)" as Bødker (1989) says, because activity theory recognizes that changing conditions can realign the constituents of an activity.

A key idea in activity theory is the notion of *mediation* (Kuutti, 1991). Artifacts, such as instruments, signs, and machines, mediate activity and are created by people to control their own behavior. Artifacts carry with them a particular culture and history (Kuutti, 1991) and are persistent structures that stretch across activities through time and space.

Distributed Cognition
The distributed cognition approach

is a new branch of cognitive science devoted to the study of: the representation of knowledge both inside the heads of individuals and in the world . . . ; the propagation of knowledge between different individuals and artifacts . . . ; and the transformations which external structures undergo when operated on by individuals and artifacts . . . . By studying cognitive phenomena in this fashion it is hoped that an understanding of how intelligence is manifested at the systems level, as opposed to the individual cognitive level, will be obtained. (Flor and Hutchins, 1991)

Distributed cognition asserts as a unit of analysis a *cognitive system* composed of individuals and the artifacts they use (Flor and Hutchins, 1991; Hutchins, 1991a). The cognitive system is closely tied to what activity theorists would call an activity; for example Hutchins (1991a) describes the activity of flying a plane, focusing on "the cockpit system." Systems have goals; in the cockpit, for example, the goal is the "successful completion of a flight." (The word *goal* in American usage is basically like what activity theorists call an *object* in that it connotes a higher-level motive.) Because the system is not relative to an individual but to a distributed collection of interacting people and artifacts, we cannot understand how a system achieves its goal by understanding "the properties of individual agents alone, no matter how detailed the knowledge of the properties of those individuals might be" (Hutchins, 1991a). The cockpit, with its pilots and instruments forming a single cognitive system, can only be understood when we understand, as a unity, the contributions of the individual agents in the system and the coordination necessary among the agents to enact the goal, that is, to achieve "the successful completion of a flight."

Distributed cognition is concerned with structure—representations inside and outside the head—and the transformations these structures undergo. This is very much in line with traditional cognitive science (Newell and Simon, 1972) but with the radical difference that access to external resources—other people and artifacts—is taken to be a crucial aspect of cognition. Because of the focus on representations—both internal to an individual and those created and displayed in artifacts—an important emphasis is on the study of such representations. Distributed cognition tends to provide finely detailed analyses of particular artifacts (Norman 1988; Norman and Hutchins, 1988; Nardi and Miller, 1990; Zhang, 1990; Hutchins, 1991a) and to be concerned with finding stable design principles that are widely applicable across design problems (Nardi and Zarmer, 1991; Norman, 1988; 1991).

The other major emphasis of distributed cognition is on understanding the coordination between individuals and artifacts; that is, to understand how individual agents align and share within a distributed process (Flor and Hutchins, 1991; Hutchins, 1991a; 1991b; Nardi and Miller, 1991). For example, Flor and Hutchins (1991) studied how two programmers performing a software maintenance task coordinated the task among themselves. Nardi and Miller (1991) studied the spreadsheet as a coordinating device facilitating the distribution and exchange of domain knowledge within an organization. In these analyses, shared goals and plans, and the particular characteristics of the artifacts in the system, are important determinants of the interactions and the quality of collaboration.

Studying Artifacts
One of the most useful aspects of activity theory and distributed cognition for studies of technology is that they emphasize the important role of artifacts in shaping activity. Leont'ev (1974) considered the use of tools to be crucial: "A tool mediates activity that connects a person not only with the world of objects, but also with other people. This means that

a person's activity assimilates the experience of humanity." Distributed cognition offers a similar notion; for example, Hutchins (1987) discusses "collaborative manipulation"—the process by which we take advantage of artifacts designed by others, sharing good ideas across time and space. Hutchins's example is a navigator using a map: the cartographer who created the map contributes, every time the navigator uses the map, to a remote collaboration in the navigator's task.

Distributed cognition studies provide in-depth analyses of artifacts such as nomograms (Norman and Hutchins, 1988), navigational tools (Hutchins, 1990b), airplane cockpits (Hutchins, 1991a), spreadsheets (Nardi and Miller, 1990; 1991), CAD systems (Petre and Green, 1991), and even everyday artifacts such as door handles (Norman, 1988). In these analyses, the artifacts are studied as they are actually used in real situations. The properties of the artifacts are seen as persisting across situations of use, and it is believed that artifacts can be designed or redesigned with respect to their intrinsic structure as well as specific situations of use. For example, a spreadsheet table is an intrinsically good design (from a perceptual standpoint) for a system in which a great deal of dense information must be displayed and manipulated in a small space (Nardi and Miller, 1990). Hutchins's (1991a) analysis of cockpit devices considers the memory requirements they impose. Norman (1988) notes whether artifacts are designed to prevent users from doing unintended (and unwanted) things with them. Petre and Green (1991) establish requirements for graphical notations for CAD users based on users' cognitive capabilities. In these studies, an understanding of artifacts is animated by observations made in real situations of their use, but there is also important consideration given to the relatively stable cognitive and structural properties of the artifacts that are not bound to a particular situation of use.

We are a long way from the ideal set out by Brooks (1991): a corpus of knowledge that identifies the properties of artifacts and situations that are most significant for design, and which permits comparison over domains, generates high level analyses, and suggests actual designs. However, there is tremendous interest and activity within the human-computer interaction community aimed toward the development of appropriate theoretical frameworks for the broad, context-based study of tasks, and it seems likely that fast progress will be made. In addition to Blomberg et al. (1992)

and Nardi (1992) for overviews, interested readers will find the papers in Floyd et al. (1992) and Engeström and Middleton (1992) valuable sources of recent work on frameworks for studying tasks and technology.

SUMMARY

The purpose of this chapter has been to ask: What is the best way to communicate with computers so that end users can have the computational power and flexibility that professional programmers enjoy? We have argued that we need not eschew formal languages as being unsuited to end users; much everyday communication is conducted via formal systems and is not at all dependent on the conversational styles of communication that we discussed in the previous chapter.

Formal end user languages may, from the user's standpoint, be textual, visual, tactile, or auditory; the sensory mode in which the user operates is not relevant. The distinction to be drawn is between a conversational style of communication in which the user "talks" to the computer (whether through voice or typed input) in his or her native language (or, more realistically, a delimited subset of that language) and a style in which the user learns a new formal language that is much closer to the native abilities of the computer. The point is to find a meeting of the minds, as it were, a common language in which both human and computer can comfortably communicate.

We must consider the motivation a person may have for doing—or not doing—a particular task. When people have an interest in performing some task, the learning and use of a formal language that describes the task simply becomes part of the activity of doing the task. Learning and use are not then problematic; for example, spreadsheet users learn the spreadsheet formula language because they are motivated to create models that establish numerical relations between the elements in their problem, and CAD users learn CAD macro languages because they want to build CAD applications.

Experience with spreadsheets and CAD systems suggests that task-specific languages are a way to provide programming power to end users, just as James Martin predicted a quarter century ago. Users who are focused on their own domain interests, and who have specific computational tasks to get done, are more likely to respond to a software system that provides high-level functionality in their area of expertise than to tolerate the slow detour of a general programming language.

We focused on task-specific end user languages as the right medium for end user programming. Like the spreadsheet formula language, such languages can be expressive and easy to learn and use. A problem with the task-specific approach is to determine just how task-specific a language should be; to some extent this depends on the circumstances under which it will be used. Careful study of those circumstances is necessary to achieve the right level of task-specificity. We suggested two theoretical frameworks for such study.

While formal task-specific languages—as opposed to natural language conversations—seem to be the technically correct way to communicate with computers, there are also social advantages to this approach. Formal end user programming languages will be much more shareable across cultures than natural language user interfaces ever could be. While there will still be differences across different writing systems, there are many fewer writing systems to support than there are natural languages (not to mention the difficulties of getting the computer to understand *any* natural language). Practically speaking, English has become the world's *lingua franca*, and languages written with English language conventions, such as the Roman alphabet and Arabic numerals, and English command names, menu labels, and so forth, will be usable by millions of people. Not everyone will use English-based systems of course, and any effort to translate a formal computer language from one set of language conventions to another will also be much easier than a parallel effort to translate a conversational user interface from one vernacular to another. Within a single human language, the vagaries of dialects, regionalisms, and speakers whose grammar is sometimes irregular (such as those for whom the language is a second language) loom as large problems for conversational human-computer communication. Such problems do not affect formal languages at all. Formal languages, then, can be seen as less parochial, less ethnocentric, and more global than a conversational style of human-computer communication. Formal languages provide users who have shared interests and needs, but different national or regional backgrounds, a common language in which to create and share applications.

4

Interaction Techniques for End User Application Development

"End User Programming: Oxymoron or Holy Grail?"
—Article by Matt Trask in *Windows Magazine*, April, 1992

We have argued that task-specificity is a cornerstone of end user programming language design. But what about visual languages, forms-based programming, programming by example, programming by example modification, and automatic program generation? These techniques have been held out as keys to end user computing, as ways to eliminate the less savory aspects of programming such as obscure syntax and reams of unreadable text with impenetrable symbols. We argue that no interaction technique in and of itself is sufficient to give end users the power they need to create their own applications; the techniques must be embedded in task-specific systems that take advantage of existing user knowledge. The problem of end user programming cannot be reduced to one of interaction technique; language design must be approached semantically.

In this chapter we examine visual languages, forms-based programming, programming by example modification, programming by example, and automatic program generation. We assess the strengths and weaknesses of each technique and try to see where each can make a contribution to end user application development.

VISUAL PROGRAMMING

Visual programming systems utilize notations that are primarily visual rather than linguistic (i.e. encoded in words). Visual programming is distinct from *program visualization*, which provides facilities for viewing

aspects of textual programs using visual means such as icons or animation; *visual programming environments*, where the language is textual
but the debugger, inspector, and so forth, may have visual elements; and
visual text editors, which support textual programming by making use
of visual techniques such as indenting, fonts, and color. Visual programming systems are often *pictorial* in nature, providing icons to represent
data and operations (e.g., systems such as LabView, HP VEE, Prograph[1]).
Some systems provide abstract visual notations based on diagrammatic
representations such as Venn diagrams (e.g., objectcharts [Bear, Coleman
and Hayes, 1989]).

Visual programming is claimed by its proponents to represent a radical
advance in the quest for solutions to the problems of end user programming. It is claimed that visual programming offers benefits in that:

- Pictures represent a higher level of abstraction, so no syntax is involved
(Myers, 1992).
- When properly designed, pictures can be understood by people regard-
less of what language they speak (Shu, 1988; Myers, 1989a; 1989b).
- Pictures can convey meaning in a more concise unit of expression than
text.
- Visual languages exploit two dimensions, which can convey more infor-
mation about structure than one-dimensional text (Myers, 1989b).

We need to take a careful look at these statements to see whether visual languages can live up to what is claimed for them. Many studies
and product descriptions catalogue a wide variety of visual programming
systems and enthusiastically proclaim their virtues (e.g., Haeberli, 1988;
Shu, 1988; Domingue, 1990; Ladret and Rueher, 1991), but unfortunately
there are few empirical studies of the actual use of visual programming
systems. However, we will consider what the literature does say about
visual languages.

Visual Notations and Naturalness

One of the strongest claims to be made about visual programming languages is that they are eminently more "natural" than textual languages—
they break through language barriers (Shu, 1988) and avoid the need to
learn syntax, instead revealing semantics through easily understood pictorial means (Myers, 1989a). These aspects would certainly represent major
advantages for end users if they were true, but there is little support for

these claims, which appear to be mostly optimistic appeals to common sense.

A key indication that claims to "naturalness" dissolve into nothing more than dogmatic assertions is that so many different programming paradigms avow naturalness, and yet none provides any evidence for such naturalness, or even says what is meant by "natural" (Green, 1990a). Green (1990a) points out that logic-based programming and object-oriented programming – opposites along some important dimensions— both claim to be "natural." Proponents of forms-based programming (Shu, 1984) and visual programming (see Myers, 1990b) also declaim the naturalness of their approach. But the empirical research, as sparse as it is, reveals a more complicated picture. For example, Detienne (1990) found that building class hierarchies with object-oriented languages is quite difficult; programmers have trouble making the most basic decisions such as whether an entity should be an object or an attribute of an object (Detienne, 1990). And Green, Petre, and Bellamy (1991) show that we cannot take the naturalness of visual programming as a given: in an experiment that tested a set of representative programming tasks, they found that performance was better using a textual language than a graphical language.

The more detailed claim that visual notations avoid the need to learn a syntax appears dubious. Syntax means rules of construction, and the need for these rules is present in any notation. Certain visual notations have been designed so that the icons used make it very clear how they can be combined (e.g., Glinert, 1989), and this is helpful. More often, however, the syntactic rules exist at the level of the construction of individual statements. The use of visual notations does not, of itself, avoid the need to construct appropriate individual statements that can involve a number of parameters. The way these parameters are specified can affect the extent to which the programmer must learn a syntax. If a syntax-directed editor is used, that will ease the process. However, textual languages can also provide syntax checking (as does the spreadsheet formula language); this is not an exclusive feature of graphical notations.

Having concluded that visual notations do not deliver miracle solutions in terms of naturalness or in doing away with syntax, we can consider how they compare with textual notations in conveying information generally.

Visual Qualities for Conveying Information

One of the main arguments for the use of visual programming notations is that they will be easier for end users to read and to understand. While pointing to the need for more research in this area, Green (1990b) cites several studies (e.g., Green, 1982; Cunniff, Taylor and Black, 1986; Cunniff and Taylor, 1987; Curtis, 1989) that cast doubt on this assertion. A number of problems have been identified in the interpretation of diagrams, and where benefits have been seen, they do not represent quantum leaps in improvement (Green, 1982). In particular, it seems that the effectiveness with which diagrams provide support to the programmer depends on the programming task (e.g., pure comprehension, inspecting structures, debugging) and on the particular style or strategies of the programmer (Green, 1982). In addition, many different factors are involved in the interpretation of diagrams and icons, including cultural background and real world knowledge, (Bernard and Marcel, 1984), making it difficult to guarantee the desired interpretation of a given diagrammatic notation.

Petre and Green (1990) suggest that visual notations can be used effectively to give programmers an overview of a program when they want to work at the highest levels of program structure. Similarly, relations and connectivity may be more easily grasped through visual representations than through textual representations. By contrast, Petre and Green (1990) highlight areas where text appears to be the best representation in terms of both information extraction and basic practical concerns. These areas include annotation, the lowest level description of statements, appendixes, and lists.

The work cited by Green (1990b) considered generic programming notations such as flowcharts or graphical versions of textual languages. The extent to which visual notations can ease program understanding when a notation is designed for a limited application domain is not known. However, Myers (1989b) and Green (1990a) point out that concurrent programs, programs for real-time control, and programs for creating graphical interfaces appear to be good candidates for graphical representation.

Practical Concerns

A serious problem for visual notations is the way they use the limited screen space of the average PC or workstation. Myers (1989b) suggests that a strength of visual programming notations is that they can use more than one dimension (programs can run across as well as down a screen). This ought to mean, in principle, that they make better use of the screen space available. However, there is an inherent problem with the use of iconic representations in that they do not support the same density of detailed information as a textual representation. Even small pieces of programs represented as icons rapidly overflow the bounds of a single screen.

This is a problem because, as was discovered in the spreadsheet study, users prefer to see as much as possible on the screen; virtually every user in the study reported that an advantage of spreadsheets is the ability to view large quantities of data on one screen (Nardi and Miller, 1990). Users had a strong preference for being able to view and access as much data as possible *without scrolling*. Many users employed screen compression programs such as SeeMORE and WideView[2] that shrink spreadsheet cells and fonts down to a very small size so that a large portion of a spreadsheet appears on a single screen. (In informal observations we have also noticed that many professional programmers use very small fonts so that as much as possible of a program appears on one screen.)

Visual clutter is a problem with iconic visual programming systems that show relations via "wires" or lines. When a system achieves any complexity, a plethora of lines crisscross the screen, obscuring rather than revealing structure. To some extent clutter may be controlled via abstraction and filtering mechanisms.

In addition to the practical problems of screen real estate and visual clutter, graphical programming languages suffer from being difficult to port (because of the graphics) and expensive to develop because of the high cost of building the necessary editors, compilers, and debuggers (Myers, 1990b).

Because the temptation to graphics is so strong, we quote a thought-provoking statement from Brooks (1987) in which he admonishes us not to search for "silver bullets" in programming:

A favorite subject for Ph.D. dissertations in software engineering is graphical, or visual, programming—the application of computer graphics to software design. Sometimes the promise held out by such an approach is postulated by analogy with VLSI chip design, in which computer graphics plays so fruitful a role. . . . Nothing even convincing, much less exciting, has yet emerged from such efforts. I am persuaded that nothing will. . . . [T]he screens of today are too small, in pixels, to show both the scope and the resolution of any seriously detailed software diagram. . . . More fundamentally, . . . software is very difficult to visualize. Whether one diagrams control flow, variable-scope nesting, variable cross-references, dataflow, hierarchical data structures, or whatever, one feels only one dimension of the intricately interlocked software elephant. If one superimposes all the diagrams generated by the many relevant views, it is difficult to extract any global overview. The VLSI analogy is fundamentally misleading—a chip design is a layered two-dimensional description whose geometry reflects its realization in 3-space. A software system is not.

The available empirical research does not support the more general claims of proponents of visual programming as far as naturalness, comprehensibility, or the elimination of syntax. And Myers (1992) notes that "visual languages do not actually help end users with the difficult *concepts* of programming such as conditionals and iteration." However, some tasks and domains appear to be well suited to visual notations such as concurrent programs, or programs for real-time control (Green, 1990b). A key drawback of visual languages is their poor use of screen real estate; to some extent this problem may be alleviated by filtering and abstraction mechanisms. Of practical concern is the expense of building editors, compilers, and debuggers (Myers, 1990b).

FORMS-BASED SYSTEMS

Since at least the mid-seventies, it has been recognized that filling out a form is an activity familiar to and easy for users who are not trained in programming (Thomas and Gould, 1975; Greenblatt and Waxman, 1978). Might not forms-based interaction techniques ease many programming burdens, giving end users greater computing power?

The answer, in a nutshell, seems to be, yes—up to a point. Jeffries and Rosenberg (1987) provide a balanced look at the costs and benefits of forms-based systems, pointing out that for many applications forms give good access to computing resources, provided the level of task complexity is not too high.

The advantages of forms-based systems are that they (1) reduce memory load and typing errors by providing at least some options on menus, (2) reduce errors by asking the user only to fill in fields rather than to construct programmatic statements whose syntax must be correct, and (3) provide a prototypic solution to a class of problems that does not need to be constructed by the user from scratch (Jeffries and Rosenberg, 1987).

However, forms-based systems lack generality, and performance degrades as the problem to be solved varies away from the prototypical solution embodied in the form (Jeffries and Rosenberg, 1987). A major limitation of forms-based systems is that they generally do not handle complex procedural tasks well. By nature they are better suited to declarative representations (Jeffries and Rosenberg, 1987).

Many forms-based systems work only for a class of problems that can be conceived of as a combination of a relatively small number of variables with associated allowable values. In FrameMaker, for example, document styles are constructed by filling in forms via dialog boxes (a type of form commonly seen in today's user interfaces) in which the user assigns values to the variables of interest. The number of styles that can be created is limited by the number of parameters offered by FrameMaker, since most parameters have a small finite set of discrete values. In a spreadsheet, by contrast, an infinite number of applications can be created (in theory anyway, not considering memory limitations, etc.) since the user has complete freedom to write formulas with any number of terms, and with an infinite range of (numeric) values. Still, there are many applications that fit well within the constraints imposed by structuring a problem as the combination of a finite number of variable values, and useful applications can be constructed using this approach.

Other forms-based systems such as OBE, or Office by Example (Zloof, 1981) provide more flexibility in allowing users to create functions (called "triggers" in OBE) that can be invoked in other forms. For example, a trigger might specify that budget amounts be checked on a daily basis for all managers, and if a manager exceeds her budget, a message should be sent to inform the manager. (See figure 4.1.) Notice that the definition of the trigger involves a condition, $E > B$, such that the user is writing a programmatic statement, not simply filling in a field with a fixed set of permissible values. In OBE, a forms-like user interface is preserved, but users are in fact writing executable statements that can be invoked from other parts of the program.

A potential problem with forms-based programming of the OBE variety is that, like the graphical programming systems we have looked at, forms are very space intensive, showing a rather small amount of information in

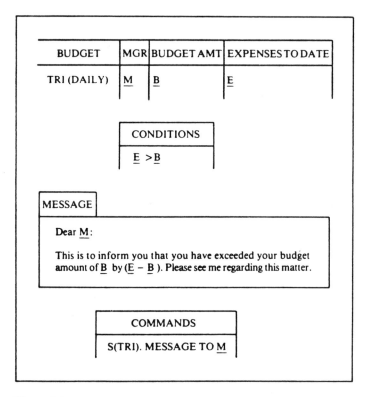

Figure 4.1
Programming in Office by Example (from Zloof, 1991, with permission of the author)

a relatively large space. This would tend to lead to difficulties if users were writing complex programs in which they needed to see a large chunk of the program at once, to check for flow of control problems, for example, or to get an overview of the program's functionality.

Computer-based forms must be well designed; in particular, it is easy to lose useful perceptual cues that readers exploit in reading paper forms (Nygren et al., 1992). In a study of the use of forms by physicians, Nygren et al. (1992) found that "The mere thickness of the bundle of papers gave an immediate indication of the case, [e.g.] 'this patient must have a chronic disease.' Yellowing of the paper and the kind of typewriter font used was effectively used to assess document age. Remembrance of position on page was used as an effective cue for searching for information which had been seen before." Nygren et al. (1992) show how the pattern of filled values against a background of unfilled space provides important cues for the reader of the form: the differing patterns are associated with various patient states.

Such cues typically disappear in computerized forms. However, with care, perceptual cues can be incorporated into computerized forms, as Nygren et al. (1992) show with their design for a form used by parts buyers at a Volvo factory in Sweden. The forms use color and fonts much as they are used in the paper forms, but more subtly (and requiring more work on the designers' part); they also preserve "values in dedicated fixed positions," which create patterns that users recognize at a glance. The forms are shown in "pads" in which thickness of the pad is shown, indicating the size of a project. The subsections of the pad are color-coded to give users an overview of the types of information found in the pad.

Forms-based systems seem most suited to relatively simple applications without complex procedural demands. Forms are useful where a problem can be readily structured as a task in which a set of variables is identified ahead of time, and users need only assign allowable values to the variables. The work of Zloof (1981) and Shu (1984) has shown that forms can be extended beyond such applications to include applications that define executable functions that can be called from within other parts of the program. Forms appear to be a useful mechanism for end user application development as evidenced by a number of applications (e.g., Zloof, 1981; Greif, 1982; Hayes and Szekeley, 1983; Postosnak, 1984; Shu 1984). The ubiquity of dialog boxes in today's software products also attests to the utility of forms. Where a good deal of procedural flexibility is wanted, forms will not be the best solution, but many applications can probably use forms for at least some tasks associated with the application. Nygren et al. (1992) provide practical advice on designing forms to preserve important perceptual cues for forms users.

PROGRAMMING BY EXAMPLE MODIFICATION

Another proposal for sidestepping the problems of writing programs in conventional languages has been to have users modify existing example programs, instead of programming from scratch (Lewis and Olson, 1987; Neal, 1989; MacLean et al., 1990). The idea is that the complexity and difficulty of general-purpose programming can be reduced by giving end users a head-start with existing code, which they then modify for their particular applications.[3]

There are two problems with this approach. First, it is not clear how users will find appropriate example code; for any practical application of example modification, many libraries of example code will have to be available, and the information access problems will be significant (see Creech, Freeze and Griss, 1991). Users will have the twin problems of searching for and recognizing apposite examples. Searching large systems is an unsolved problem, and users' lack of familiarity with the programming language in which examples are written would seem to make it difficult for users to recognize appropriate examples even if they were actually looking at them. Second, we think that conventional programming languages, no matter how well supported, are not appropriate for the large population of users who lack intrinsic interest in computers and have very specific jobs to accomplish. These users should be supported at their level of interest, which is to perform specific computational tasks, not to become computer programmers. Thus we see task-specific end user programming languages, such as the spreadsheet formula language, as superior to efforts to ease the learning and use of general programming languages.

What about programming by modifying domain-specific examples? This solution still does not solve the problem of having to depend on the existence of appropriate example code. True end user programming systems allow users to build a meaningful application without reliance on obtaining code from other more sophisticated users. No programmer wants to lack the skills with which to create a program from scratch, since that is so often necessary. If it is impossible to begin a program without an existing program, the user is denied real control over the computational environment. Also, it is not clear whether users who modify existing example programs could ever really come to understand the programs they modify. Without a firm grasp of the language in which the examples are written, the ability to modify a program to suit one's needs would seem very limited.

There is a need to draw a distinction between programming by modifying example programs and the reuse of software modules. Reusable software modules are clearly desirable. CAD users extensively reuse existing code (Tee, 1992). In the spreadsheet world there is software reuse in the form of templates used by groups of users (Nardi and Miller, 1991). A template is a framework for an entire spreadsheet in which all parameters and formulas have been specified and the user must fill in the appropriate data values. For example, a financial officer might distribute a spreadsheet template to the managers of the departments that report to her, so that she gets standardized budget reporting.

Spreadsheet users find templates useful, but they are not dependent on them, and they routinely create their own applications using the spreadsheet formula language. We asked users what they liked about spreadsheets, and several users reported that they can be "creative" with spreadsheets, that it is "easy" to build their own models. One user captured a general feeling about spreadsheets in noting that he thinks of the spreadsheet as a "blank canvas"—a medium in which to directly express his own thoughts—just the opposite of an artifact created by someone else that must be reworked before it is of any use.

The large variety of applications modeled with spreadsheets (Lewis and Olson, 1987; Nardi and Miller, 1991) does indeed suggest a blank canvas. Spreadsheet applications include mathematical modeling (Arganbright, 1986), simple databases, managing small businesses, forecasting trends, analyzing scientific and engineering data, and of course the financial applications for which they were first intended. Users have programmed these diverse and sometimes sophisticated applications without the aid of example programs.

PROGRAMMING BY EXAMPLE

An innovative approach to the problems of end user programming is that of programming by example. Programming by example proponents argue that people are good at thinking concretely but less good at abstractions such as those involved in programming. A solution to the problem of end user programming, then, is to allow users to specify examples.

In programming by example systems, the user supplies a concrete example, through direct manipulation techniques, and the system infers or "induces" a program from the example by detecting a pattern in the user's actions. The actions might map, for example, to an operation such as "iterate."[4]

Let's look at a typical programming by example scenario. Cypher (1991) sketched a scenario for his programming by example system, Eager, in which a HyperCard user wants to collect all the subject headings from her mail messages in a HyperCard stack and place them on one card, a "Subject List." She copies the subject heading from the first card to the Subject List. She copies the heading from the second card to the Subject List. By now the system has caught on that she wants *all* the headings from the stack to be entered onto the Subject List. The system performs this action for her. Instead of the user having to write an iterative loop to get all the headings onto the Subject List, the system has inferred her intention from the concrete actions that she took. The actions have the advantage of being familiar direct manipulation HyperCard operations. The system then writes a HyperTalk script to do the loop.

In another scenario (from Myers, 1990a), the user creates a graphical object in a window. He then creates another object of the same type. He moves the two objects so that they are vertically aligned at the distance he wishes. When the next object of the same type is created, it is properly aligned with respect to the first two.[5]

Such scenarios have immense appeal. They hint at fulfilling the promise of computers as truly intelligent machines. But there are problems with programming by example techniques. Though they are useful for solving certain limited user programming problems within specific domains, they are unlikely to be a general solution to the user programming problem.

What are the problems with programming by example systems? In a nutshell, they lack the ability to clearly express terminating conditions and branching—two fundamental programming capabilities; they do not accomodate our natural exploratory behavior; and they incorrectly distribute processing and programming effort. We discuss each of these problems in turn.

Setting Boundaries and Expressing Conditions

Programming by example systems have difficulty establishing termination conditions (i.e., setting boundaries for the execution of a program instruction) (Cypher, 1991). In our HyperCard example, what if the user wanted the message headings from seven different stacks, out of her total collection of twenty-five stacks, to be entered onto the Subject List? Would she have to do two iterations on each of seven stacks before the system understood what she intended? In another scenario, Myers (1990a) suggested that, "The user might drag a file named 'v1.ps' to the trash can, and then a file named 'v2.ps,' and a [programming by example] system might automatically create a macro to delete all files that end in '.ps'." But why not delete all files starting with v? Or all files starting with v and ending with .ps? Or all files starting with v followed by a numeral? Or all files beginning with a v followed by a numeral and ending in .ps? And from which folders are the files to be deleted? It is as much a problem for the *user* to figure out what patterns the system might be able to understand so that he can predict its behavior as it is for the system to gain enough knowledge to infer the correct pattern. Cypher (1991) used this very example of file deletion to illustrate the boundary problem, stating, "A user expecting a [programming by example] system to delete all of the documents in the current folder would be shocked to observe it blithely deleting all of the documents on the disk!" The inevitable imprecision of generalizing from individual examples (and a small number at that, if programming by example is not to be too tedious) would seem to prove most frustrating to users trying to figure out what the system will actually do.

It is difficult to imagine a robust, general programming by example facility for handling conditionals. What if our HyperCard user wanted the system to collect all the headings except headings indicating birthday greetings (from her recent birthday)? Or, take Myers's (1991) description of specifying heading styles in documents by supplying examples. The user creates a heading in the format he wants, and then the system applies the format to all other headings. Myers notes, however, that if a heading is too long and runs over onto the next line, the heading style specified by the example does not work. While under at least some restricted conditions a system can reasonably be expected to detect, or be instructed to perform, a series of repetitive actions via the input of concrete physical actions, the situation is much more complicated for conditionals. The wide scope of possible conditions relevant to performing a given action, as well as the difficulty of instructing the system about conditions through concrete examples, argue against the general feasibility of programming by example systems supplying conditionals. We also suspect that a huge programming effort would be needed to supply this kind of capability, even for very specific cases within a restricted domain. An effort of this sort should consider the trade-offs of designing and implementing automatic programming capabilities versus providing task-specific ways to give users direct access to conditionals, such as those provided in textual form in the spreadsheet formula language.

The question of supporting conditional statements via programming by example techniques is still, of course, open to further research. Cypher (1991) plans extensions to Eager that will provide conditionals. He notes that the interaction techniques will be different than those for specifying iterative actions. His future work will be of interest.

Pattern Matching and Random Actions
Maulsby, Witten and Kittlitz (1989) discussed another set of problems with programming by example systems. Citing Maulsby's (1988) study of MacDraw users, the authors noted that " . . . performing a set of graphical tasks . . . revealed that execution traces are riddled with extraneous and erroneous actions. Users not only made mistakes, but were observed performing experiments or simply fidgeting. The order of actions varied greatly within the first several iterations of loops."

This certainly sounds like the way people actually behave! Because people make mistakes, do things differently from one time to the next, go off on tangents doing experiments, and just generally fool around, induction programs have to be that much smarter to infer users' intentions. Maulsby, Witten and Kittlitz (1989) argue that programs can only be smart up to a point about human foibles, and that users must be trained to constrain their behavior in ways that inhibit random or exploratory behavior. Their "Metamouse" graphics program, a programming by example system, trains users in techniques adapted from teaching arithmetic to young children. Users behave like teachers with respect to the system, applying techniques for "training" the system to learn what they want it to know. Users of the system are supposed to "adopt an intentional stance toward the system"; that is, they should refrain from the extraneous and erroneous actions Maulsby (1988) found in his study of MacDraw users.

The idea of the "intentional stance" raises the question of how much we should expect users to change the way they behave in order to be able to use a system that is supposed to be making life easier for them. Doing experiments, even fidgeting to relax a bit, might be considered beneficial behaviors that we do not want to inhibit. Errors are inevitable. Though programming by example is intended to eliminate some of the tedium and restrictiveness of using traditional programming languages, it may, in some cases, have hidden costs in forcing users to reduce some of the random activity that we habitually engage in.

The lack of strict procedure in our everyday problem-solving activities is especially problematic when we consider using programming by example techniques to produce longer programs that involve more than just a few steps. Often we perform a sequence of actions incorrectly, or forget something that should have happened several steps ago, or we create procedures on the fly, critiquing our efforts as we go. We may not know what all of the relevant steps of a procedure should be, and we work incrementally and experimentally, rather than laying out entire procedures in advance (Bar-On, Or-Bach, and Ranney, 1991; Nardi and Zarmer, 1991). This kind of problem solving is very productive but is not supported by programming by example because the system needs carefully patterned information to perform the inferencing correctly. Since current programming by example systems do not permit the direct editing of a script or program, an "incorrect" example must be executed again from scratch if the system is to be able to detect the pattern correctly.

Creating programming by example systems appears to be a difficult programming task, even for systems in limited domains. Maulsby, Witten and Kittlitz (1989), Myers (1990a) and Cypher (1991) argue that programming by example systems will work best within restricted domains. However, even in the restricted domains within which their research prototypes are actually implemented, difficult, sophisticated programming techniques are used to make the inferencing work correctly. For example, Metamouse (Maulsby, Witten and Kittlitz, 1989) is based on STRIPS-like theorem proving (Fikes and Nilsson, 1971), as well as NODDY, a robot programming language (Andreae, 1985). Myers (1990a) remarked: "It is relatively difficult to implement [programming by example systems]."

Since it is expensive and difficult to create programming by example systems, a basic question about them is: Why not simply provide a direct command (or set of programmable commands) that the user uses to tell the system what to do, instead of requiring the system to *infer intention* from user actions? The "create an example" part of the programming by example approach can be pulled out and used without an inference engine (Myers, 1990b). If the user signals an intention to perform an action instead of requiring the system to infer intention, the inferencing-related costs of development and processing can be eliminated.

Let's look at two systems that help users with iteration. Cypher's (1991) Eager system helps users perform repetitive tasks within a HyperCard stack (at least those restricted to a simple pattern). Likewise, spreadsheets allow users to iterate operations over blocks of cells through direct manipulation techniques. In both cases, the tedium of writing programming loops in a general programming language and the need to understand the loop as a programming abstraction—instead of as a repetition of a concrete, familiar task—are avoided. In both cases, this is a happy state of affairs for the user. But in the programming by example system, a greater burden is added to the computer as it must infer user intentions (which the spreadsheet does not have to do). Is this burden really necessary?

We believe that in many or most cases, inferring user intentions is not necessary. Users can gain all the benefits of having a program perform some action for them (such as the iteration) without the cost of the continual monitoring. For example, in the case of the multiple HyperCard stacks that we sketched above, it would seem to be easier for the user to give an example on one stack and then give the other stacks as arguments. The user could indicate that she wants to initiate an iteration and then go through the first two iterations, signaling that they constitute the desired action. The program does not have to watch for this. No inferencing need be done across the stacks either, because the user can simply tell the system which stacks to go through. These arguments could be supplied through simple point-and-click actions. The system would need detailed knowledge of its objects and operations to complete the iteration, but there would be no need for a complex inferencing mechanism that constantly watches in the background for patterned actions.

Cypher (1991) reported that in his user study of Eager, "all users were uncomfortable with giving up control when Eager took over." Cypher made two modifications to Eager to deal with this problem—saving a copy of a stack that is going to be modified by Eager, and providing a stepping mode that allows users to confirm each action. However, it seems that the problem could be solved more simply by having users directly control the system's actions, (as suggested above, using direct manipulation techniques), avoiding the need to provide inferencing, and at the same time giving users the control that they want. User confirmation of each action is moving in that direction anyway, with users taking a more active role in program execution.

Myers (1990a) argued that adding commands to a system—which eliminates the need for inferencing—would increase the number of commands for users, and might require programming knowledge that end users do not have. However, presumably the commands that would be added to the system would be those commonly used, so added learning time would be cost-effective. Any extra learning time would be more than offset by the problems users would have when the system incorrectly inferred their actions and created incorrect procedures. With no way into the program, users can do no troubleshooting and have no means of error correction.

With respect to error correction, Myers (1990a) noted that one experimental study of spreadsheets showed that many user-generated procedures for spreadsheets are incorrect (Brown and Gould, 1987), and that therefore "it will be interesting to see whether procedures that are [induced through examples], or programmed by end users are more reliable in practice." However, in our spreadsheet study we found that users devote considerable attention to debugging spreadsheets, and errors that make a difference in the correct use of a spreadsheet are usually eliminated. Debugging is accomplished cooperatively, with different users checking and cross-checking one another's work (Nardi and Miller, 1991). The Brown and Gould (1987) study that Myers (1990a) cited was conducted under strict experimental conditions, and though users certainly did make plenty of mistakes in their spreadsheets, they had no opportunity to perform the kind of debugging that we found in our study. We think it unlikely that error correction will be easier in programming by example systems.

It is true, as Myers (1990a) says, that some commands added to the user interface might require programming knowledge that users do not have. However, it is unrealistic to expect that people can use a system without some investment in learning. To reduce learning effort as much as possible, commands must be designed and chosen with care. Commands that map as closely as possible onto the task-specific operations that users want to perform in their applications will support users at their level of skill and interest. Task-specific commands avoid the problem of being at such a low level that detailed, unfamiliar programming knowledge is required.

Despite the limits and problems of the programming by example approach, we think that there is a role for specific programming by example techniques within larger programs. Cypher's (1991) Eager system shows how useful functionality can be supplied via programming by example within the context of a specific program. Programming by example techniques by themselves, however, will not solve the problem of giving end users the power to write complex domain specific applications. The difficulty of expressing terminating conditions and conditionals, the need to inhibit random/exploratory user actions, the lack of error correction mechanisms, and the high cost of the inferencing capabilities of programming by example systems make offering real computing power to end users via these techniques quite difficult. A challenge for the future is to determine how to fit specific programming by example techniques into larger programs that offer power and flexibility to end users.

AUTOMATIC PROGRAMMING BY INFORMAL PROGRAM SPECIFICATION

When considering how to provide end users with a system with which to generate applications, a utopian approach of interest is that of automatic program generation. One can imagine a futuristic system that accepts information about requirements for the program from the user in a form that is natural and familiar, interprets the requirements, and automatically generates a program to meet the requirements. In such a system, the learning and effort of the user is minimized, and a major burden is placed on the computer system. The model of the interaction is less that of a programmer with a compiler and more that of a client with a systems analyst. In considering this approach to end user program creation, difficulties can be anticipated that have implications for both the design of the user-system dialogue and for the technology required to implement such a system (Rousseau, 1990). Three key areas are:

1. The means of specifying requirements,
2. The form of human-computer communication used,

3. The evaluation of resulting programs and the identification of requirements.

Requirements Specification

If one assumes that the system will be driven by users' specifications of their requirements (the issue of how users arrive at their requirements is discussed below), one must consider how these requirements will be formulated. A study of dialogues with designers (Rousseau, 1990) established that much of the specification process involved describing the user interface or external behavior of the desired program. The fact that end users are better able to describe such concrete, dynamic behavior than abstract, static code has been commented on elsewhere (Lau-Kee, 1990). This suggests, therefore, that end users should be given an interface that allows them to communicate the form of the desired program in a similarly concrete manner in terms of the behavior they wish to obtain.

Two possible approaches to this can be considered. The first involves users communicating program behavior by demonstrating it, as discussed in the previous section. The other approach is to imagine a system where the user can describe program behavior using means of communication that are considerably less prescribed than traditional programming languages. Simply using a specification language as many existing automatic programming systems do (e.g., Blumofe and Hecht, 1988), is, in reality, doing little more than replacing one programming language by another as far as the end user is concerned. Under those circumstances, traditional problems of language design will arise.

If one avoids the use of a fixed programming language, another problem arises. The advantage of using a programming language is that it serves the dual function of defining the means of user-system communication and of informing the user, in a detailed manner, of which facilities are available; if there is no word for this function in the language, then it must not be provided. In the absence of a programming language, as such, other means must be found for communicating the tasks that a program can support, the form programs can take, and the particular facilities that are available. Two studies of how users make use of information of this kind in generating program specifications to meet their requirements discovered that such information is used in a very informal and imprecise manner (Rousseau, 1990).

In one study, subjects were presented with a number of screens from an electronic diary, instructed to treat the screens as fixed, and asked to describe functions or commands that they would like to accompany the screens. While many of the comments did describe desired functions, 38 out of 85 comments related to changes to the screens rather than functions. Some requests were for facilities that were outside of what had been defined as possible.

In the other study (also reported in Rousseau, 1990), university research staff were asked about the way they store and access lists of references to papers and books. The researchers were provided with a description of a set of programming facilities that were available to them (based on a subset of HyperCard) and an example stack. They were asked to specify how they would like a computer-based reference database to be designed using these facilities. For the users with no experience with HyperCard, the description alone proved difficult to understand and use as a basis for designing a system. The example stack left subjects unclear about what was fixed and what could be changed. As with the previous study, the subjects would, on occasion, request a facility that was outside of what had been defined as possible.

Further research is required to identify which manipulations of the instructions will reduce the proportion of inappropriate specifications. However, it is clear that the users are not readily able to generate requirements that strictly fit the constraints presented to them. It is hypothesized that two processes are involved; one of generating ideas for requirements combined with another of assessing their appropriateness. The information given to users of automatic programming systems will need to support both of these processes.

The Form of Communication

In addition to problems at the macro level of means of communication, problems will also exist at the micro level, if the approach of informally communicating a program specification is to be attempted.

While there are many who would have no hesitation in advocating the use of "natural language" as the means of user-system communication for automatic program generation, we do not believe that a natural language interface is an appropriate solution. There may be a language that is "natural" to users in the sense that it is familiar and in common usage, but it is very likely that this language would be distressingly unnatural to the computer. "Naturalness," *in toto*, is a function of the relationship between the system language, the users' language abilities, the communication task in question, and the computer's abilities, including hardware capabilities (see Rich, 1985; Buxton, 1987).

What is required, then, if informal program specification is to be a possibility, is a more structured approach than free prose; that is, an approach that is prejudicial to neither the human nor the computer. While there is no ideal solution to the communication problem, some possible solutions are form-filling interfaces, restricted, task-specific languages such as the spreadsheet formula language, structured notations such as flowcharting (see Rousseau, 1992a), and even drawing tools. WorldBuilder,[6] for example, uses a combination of such communicative forms. Screen designs and layouts are communicated using drawing tools, properties of objects or characters are defined using form-filling interfaces, and program behavior is specified using a fairly conventional textual programming language. The programming language requires the most learning on the part of users.

Evaluation and the Identification of Requirements

No matter what form of communication is chosen for program specification, inevitably there will be points of miscommunication. It will be important, therefore, for the system to present users with its interpretation of their requirements. Possibly the best means of doing this is by generating a candidate program. Users would then evaluate the program, and further dialogue would be in order to iron out any misunderstandings and achieve a program closer to users' requirements. This is implied in techniques used in programming by example systems such as Smallstar in which the user demonstrates the desired program and is then given the code generated by the computer to edit further (see Lau-Kee, 1990).

The other motivation behind such a dialogue is the observation that end users are often much better at identifying and communicating their needs if they have a concrete program to criticize, rather than working with abstract requirements or specifications (Harwood, 1987; Nardi and Zarmer, 1991). The findings of Nardi and Zarmer (1991) suggest that users incrementally develop successive versions of their programs to help them in understanding their own requirements. Rousseau's (1990) study of users specifying requirements to developers found a similar opportunistic, bottom-up approach. Even skilled designers appear to engage in an iterative, opportunistic process when generating designs or specifications (Guindon, 1988; Visser, 1990; Davies, 1991). The best approach to designing the dialogue of such a system, then, would involve a short, initial specification dialogue that serves to identify the rough class of program required, with the main dialogue being based around a series of proposed programs or prototypes.

Whatever form the dialogue takes, there will be a need for users to assess the proposed program against their needs. How should this be done? Presenting users with raw program code to evaluate is unlikely to be helpful. Some means of presenting the program in the form in which the user would actually interact with it (possibly a prototype) would probably be most suitable. It would be desirable to make the editing/criticizing process as similar to the original specification process as possible (Lau-Kee, 1990). Perhaps the best approach would be one in which the initial specification dialogue is short and serves to identify the rough class of program required, while the main work of communication occurs around a series of proposed programs.

A study of the evaluation behavior of users when presented with a potentially useful diary program has been carried out to examine this problem (Rousseau, 1992b). It was observed that users tended to focus on the facilities provided by the program rather than on its support for their task needs. Getting users to describe the task needs prior to the evaluation reduced this effect, however. Also, data from customer behavior (Fletcher, 1987) indicate that when assessing complex products such as video recorders, customers attempt to simplify the assessments by focusing on a small number of factors. These studies suggest points at which users have difficulty in the evaluation process.

Further evidence to support the view that the evaluation process in automatic programming would be problematic comes from the work of experts in user testing of system prototypes. The experience in this area indicates that effective and thorough evaluations will only take place if a number of factors are considered and a procedure is followed. Thus, subjects should not just examine the prototype but should perform sample tasks using the prototype (Eason, 1988). Also, there may be an element of skill involved in spotting points where the performance is indicative of poor design (Wright and Monk, 1989).

Another practical problem is that users may not be able to identify fundamental problems early on, so that the degree of reworking of the program that is required after each evaluation could be considerable. This, in turn, could lead to a rather lengthy period of iteration. However, Nardi and Zarmer (1991) found that spreadsheet users with three to five years of experience *were* able to incrementally develop and evaluate their programs. Users discovered needs as they went along, and the interaction with the spreadsheet package directly supported this vital process. Evaluation seems most feasible if it takes place in the context of developing an understanding of requirements, rather than simply being presented with a program "cold" and having to match it to some imaginary set of requirements.

The need to work within a development context in which needs can be discovered suggests a fundamental problem with automatic programming systems for end users. The utopian picture is that of a system so advanced that users have merely to tell it what they want, and it will build it for them. If, however, users do not know what they want, then such a system might prove intractable. If users cannot give a description of the desired program, nor describe their requirements, nor effectively evaluate any programs generated by the system, then the dialogue envisaged will fail to provide the appropriate support. We would argue, therefore, that the time-consuming struggle of iteratively and incrementally developing programs is a necessary and irreplaceable component of any end user programming activity. Rather than attempting to provide tools that avoid the need for incrementally working through problems, it will be more fruitful to develop tools that make the struggle as short, attractive, and productive as possible. Spreadsheets have succeeded in doing this to a considerable degree (see Nardi and Zarmer, 1991).

While one can conceive of a system that could automatically generate programs for end users, the probability of such a system producing right-the-first-time programs appears to be low. There may well be a role for high-level programming languages and environments that enable users to specify programs, evaluate them, and iterate toward desirable ones. These will probably not deliver the miracle of "automatic programming" that one might hope for, however. Such systems must be left to the science fiction writers.

SUMMARY

We have tried to show that it is tempting but unhelpful to search for silver bullets as we seek solutions to the problems of end user programming. Many interaction techniques have been heralded as *the* answer. But upon inspection we find that these techniques all have their limitations. And no single technique by itself addresses the semantic issue of designing a programming language that taps into user knowledge and leverages users' skills, interests, and familiarity with their domains to make programming more interesting and intelligible. However, any of these techniques may prove useful as a local solution to a problem of user interaction within a task-specific language.

More empirical research is needed on existing systems to expose their strengths and weaknesses. The existing empirical studies such as Mackay, (1990), MacLean et al., (1990), Cypher, (1991), Nardi and Miller (1990; 1991), Petre and Green (1991) and Tee (1992) provide an idea of what can be learned about existing end user programming systems and the approaches to follow in conducting empirical research. Brooks (1991) has suggested that a taxonomy of interaction techniques and the problems each technique solves would go a long way toward design "reuse." If such a taxonomy were available, designers would not have to start from scratch with each new system design but could find out how similar problems have been solved in the past. At this point, with so little practical experience and empirical research, it is impossible to provide a taxonomy that suggests which techniques and approaches will work well for which set of problems. Creating such a taxonomy will be a fruitful line of study for future research.

5
Visual Application Frameworks

The baseball box score is the pithiest form of written communication in America today. It is two or three hours . . . of complex activity, virtually inscribed on the head of a pin.

—Fred Schwed, Jr., quoted in *Baseball by the Rules*

As we have noted, many very workable end user programming languages—the spreadsheet formula language, CAD macro languages, the languages used in statistical packages and Mathematica—are primarily *textual*. The advantages of text, that is, terseness and low development and processing cost, have been noted. What, then, should be the role of visualization in end user programming language design? We believe that many successful end user programming systems will be *hybrid* systems, managing a balanced combination of text and graphics. As Green (1990b) and Petre and Green (1990) have observed, text and graphics each have their own special strengths and weaknesses, and the best strategy is to exploit each according to its particular characteristics. There is no general recipe for doing this, but in this chapter we take a close look at three systems that combine text and graphics to create end user programming environments. An analysis of these systems gives us some exemplars to study and evaluate. We look at spreadsheets, the Logo language, and CAD systems. We also consider the use of visual formalisms as reusable visual application frameworks.

HYBRID VISUAL PROGRAMMING IN SPREADSHEETS

Having described some of the costs and benefits of visual programming, we will look at spreadsheets as an example of a hybrid system that effectively combines text and graphics. In particular, we consider the way a simple graphic object—the spreadsheet table—organizes computation for spreadsheet users. The table is used in conjunction with the textual formula language, creating a "hybrid visual programming" system.

In spreadsheets, graphics and text are each used to solve different problems. The graphics handle making program state visible (showing current values of cell variables in the table), and the textual formula language provides a compact formalism for writing program instructions. Hybrid visual programming is not iconic or pictorial in nature but uses graphics to display program state, rather than to represent operations and data flow. Nor is hybrid visual programming the same as program visualization; it is much more than mere visualization, because the textual language in which program statements are written incorporates graphical elements from the display as language primitives, as we discuss in detail below.

The compactness of a textual language permits users to write complex formulas in a very small space, leaving most of the screen free to display program state. In addition to the compactness of textual languages—an advantage that can hardly be overstated given the size of our computer screens[1] — it is (arguably) easier to read and comprehend a textual representation of formulas, such as this formula from one of our user's spreadsheets:

G22/(G7 - 750000) * I2

than a corresponding graphic representation, for example, a network with nodes representing variables and operators.

Not only do spreadsheets provide a good division of labor between text and graphics, they also provide a careful *integration* of text and graphics. Though formulas are textual, they are organized by the tabular grid, in that each formula belongs to a cell in the table. The spreadsheet thus associates a visual object, the cell itself, with a small textual program, the formula. The cells are arranged in a predictable, comprehensible pattern in the two-dimensional space of the table; hence the programs associated with the cells are also thus arranged. Here we see a true marriage of text and graphics. Program code, itself textual, is distributed over a visual grid, providing a system of compact, comprehensible, easily located program modules.

More generally, the spreadsheet table provides an overall organizing framework of rows, columns, and cells within which users organize the components of computation: parameters, variables, formulas, and subparts of their models. The table is a graphical form into which primarily textual information is placed: formulas, data values, and labels. An individual cell represents a single variable. The table provides a simple but useful relational semantics in graphical form: rows and columns are used to represent the main parameters of a model, and ranges of cells can represent subparts of a model. By leaving empty cells between ranges, a model can be visually segmented. In our study, we found that users segment spreadsheets by such criteria as years, months, geographic regions, companies, and departments.

The importance of the two-dimensional grid that arranges program components is illustrated in a conversation with Jennifer. We were discussing a spreadsheet that contained about three hundred rows and we asked her how she "gets around" in this large spreadsheet. Notice that in the following exchange she thinks we want to know the mechanics of navigating with mouse and keyboard. She adds the comment about the geometric layout of her spreadsheet as a clarification, though we have not talked about layout at any time in her interviews:

Interviewer: Now when you're actually using a spreadsheet this big, how do you get around to the places you want to be?

Jennifer: I use the mouse on the gray bar. It lets you leap down a page. It's kind of like page-up and page-down. But I can page-right and -left more easily than you can with the keyboard.

Interviewer: OK, so that's not really an issue. Even though you do have a lot of data, it's pretty easy to find it.

Jennifer: UmmHmm. I'm so familiar with the spreadsheet too, that I know that if I'm here [points to a place on the spreadsheet] in Municipal Bonds, that I know I'm in the middle of the document, and I know that Preferred Stocks is above that, and I know that Collateralized Mortgage Obligations are below that. So depending on what the next transaction is, I know whether to go up or down.

Jennifer thinks of her spreadsheets in terms of their basic components spatially arrayed in the table. The transactions expressed in the formulas are easy for her to find as the components of her financial models ("Collateralized Mortgage Obligations," etc.) are laid out in a spatial configuration that she can readily remember and navigate.

The following comment by "Betty" indicates the ease with which users associate visual objects (the cells) with program components (variables and formulas):

Betty: [I can easily see where the week's sales are.] It's very easy for me to punch in a formula there, to total up the sales for the week. . . . I figure out where the week starts, and it starts in cell three, and it ends in cell thirty. So I say, "Sum everything in between three and thirty."

Betty easily maps sales to cells; the grid structure provides a convenient way to organize data and a logical place to "punch in" a formula.

Another means of articulating graphical and linguistic information in spreadsheets is assigning names to cell ranges. In our study, some users assigned range names in large spreadsheets and then located the range by typing in the name, rather than scrolling to it. The table gives a basic graphic organization to a spreadsheet program and can be navigated by both logical (named ranges) and spatial (scrolling) means, enabling users to manage even very large spreadsheets.[2]

The table is also useful in providing a scheme for naming variables. Users do not have to name spreadsheet variables as they are prenamed according to their place in the table (e.g., A1, D2, where letters identify columns and numbers identify rows). Though seemingly a small convenience, users frequently complain of the tedium of coming up with variable names. Lewis and Olson (1987) regard this bothersome chore as a barrier to programming for many end users.

An important aspect of the use of a graphic in spreadsheets is that the program state displayed in the table is automatically updated (see Kay, 1984; Hutchins, Hollan and Norman, 1986; Lewis and Olson, 1987; Nardi and Miller, 1991). Users love the immediacy of the "twinkling lights" of the spreadsheet's instant update (Nardi and Miller, 1991). This important feedback lets users know what has changed in their model and provides a kind of instant gratification that is very satisfying.

We have looked at how the spreadsheet table organizes computation by providing a two-dimensional grid across which computational elements are arrayed. There is another important aspect of the articulation of text and graphics in spreadsheets: the formula language *understands the components of the spreadsheet table,* that is, cells and ranges of cells. There is a close coupling between the formula language (which itself is entirely textual) and a graphic object (i.e., the table) in that formula primitives are also table primitives. Formula notation expresses relations modeled graphically in the table. To return to our previous example, in the formula SUM(C1..C8), the semantics of the formula are in part *expressed in terms of the components of the table:* variables (C1..C8) are described as specific cells in the table.[3] Users find this scheme quite easy to follow. As Betty remarked, "I say, 'Sum everything in between three and thirty.'" A range of cells encompassing several rows and/or columns (or portions of them) can also be expressed in the formula notation, for example, E5..H7, where E5 is the top left corner of the rectangular range and H7 the bottom right. Even a range across several different spreadsheets can be specified, for example, SUM(B:A1..K:D4) sums the values in the A1..D4 range in spreadsheets B through K. This use of graphical forms as elements of a programming language gives users a concrete representation of variables that is readily comprehensible. It also provides a means of supporting iteration, as in the SUM example, which could be written as a loop, and in copying formulas (see Chapter 3).

Problems of Organizing Code in a Table

While distributing code across a grid is helpful to end users, there are also problems with this kind of scheme. Spreadsheets are difficult to debug. They do not lend themselves to easy reuse of individual modules within a single spreadsheet. It is hard to understand formulas in someone else's spreadsheet. Though the general intent of a spreadsheet is usually clear from the way the rows and columns are laid out, understanding individual formulas requires patience and sometimes a lengthy process of manual checking.

In our study, users' number one complaint about spreadsheets was the difficulty of debugging (Nardi and Miller, 1991). It is difficult to get a global sense of the structure of an individual formula that may have dependencies spread out all over the spreadsheet table.[4] Users have to track down individual cell dependencies one by one, tacking back and forth all over the spreadsheet. As one user, Ray, described his debugging activities, "You got a tremendous amount of formulas ... that are pointing all kinds of different directions, and you know, it's a pretty big pass to kind of walk back through the whole thing. So you have to be very careful." This situation is not helped by the fact that spreadsheets do not provide support for visualizing cell dependencies across a model. We can imagine, for example, mechanisms by which a user debugs a particular formula by bringing up a view of the spreadsheet in which irrelevant rows and columns are filtered out, and related cells are highlighted or colored. In response to our suggesting such a mechanism, Ray remarked, "Yeah, yeah. And, actually, if [such a tool] was easy to use, we wouldn't have to have a very sophisticated spreadsheet for me to want to use it. It would be a quick way to assess . . . what the dependencies are." Our users also described awkward pencil and paper procedures for recording cell values as they went through a formula debugging each element. An automated way of keeping track of this kind of information during debugging would be helpful.

Because of the distribution of code across the grid, spreadsheets are not particularly modular. Since the code that implements a particular piece of a spreadsheet is distributed over a potentially large and unpredictable set of cells, it is difficult to reuse an individual piece of one spreadsheet in another new spreadsheet. As we discussed, reuse occurs mainly in the form of templates, in which the entire template is reused, rather than modular pieces (see Nardi and Miller, 1991).

Spreadsheets are often used and shared by different users, so it is important to be able to really understand others' formulas (see Nardi and Miller, 1991 for a description of cooperative debugging practices). "Laura" described a situation in which the twin problems of debugging formulas and understanding formulas developed by others came together, creating a tedious chore for her. Laura had received a spreadsheet from her company's parent company that she was responsible for verifying. To verify formulas, she had to write everything down.

Laura: Well, they [the parent company] said in their instructions that it [the spreadsheet] hadn't been tested and if there were any formula errors it was our responsibility.

. . .

Interviewer: Okay, so you really are responsible for making sure that the formulas work then.

Laura: UmHmm. And you know, there might be formula errors or [there might not].

Interviewer: Did you find formula errors when you got [into it]?

Laura: Uh huh. . . . Actually, I only found one or two; it wasn't that many [but I still had to do all that checking]. . . . I spent *days* [checking everything]. . . . Literally days going forward and backward, just like this [she follows some formulas in her spreadsheet, jumping to the relevant cells]. . . . Writing the stuff down and saying, "Okay, what are they trying to do here?" . . . Because I do have a real good theoretical understanding and I know what the relationships are [I am able to do this].

Laura's comments point out the fact that debugging others' spreadsheets involves not only checking actual data values but also following the logic of a set of formulas. She noted that because of her "good theoretical understanding" she is able to correctly track the logic. We can imagine debugging tools that support this aspect of debugging—perhaps separate from checking arithmetical correctness—as a useful addition to spreadsheet software.

The problems of spreadsheets created by arraying small program modules across a grid are similar to the problems created by the application of object-oriented programming techniques. In object-oriented systems, the code for a particular object is distributed, invisibly, over many objects and their methods (see Berlin, 1990). Cells that participate in spreadsheet formulas are distributed across the spreadsheet table. The root cause of the difficulty in both cases is the same: the useful modularity of cells or slots lies in their being small, fine-grained units, but when it comes time to get a more global view of a particular object (with all its inherited methods and data variables), or a formula (with all its constituent cell variables), the small units that provide concreteness and modularity become a hindrance to grasping the distributed content of an object or formula. Thus, a strength of spreadsheets—the ability to build models through creating small pieces of code assembled out of specific cells—is also a weakness, just as the strength of inheritance in object-oriented systems creates some problems as well as providing useful functionality.

Green (1990a) notes that HyperCard has a similar fault/virtue in that program fragments written in HyperTalk are attached to screen objects. While this strategy breaks coding down into more manageable pieces,

Green observes that, "the overall visibility of the program has been very seriously reduced, [e.g.] you can't easily see the scripts for two buttons at the same time ..."

It seems likely that the problems of distributed code can be managed by tools that support mechanisms such as filtering, abstraction, and annotation. In this way the strengths of providing a visual framework such as the spreadsheet table can be preserved, while the deficits of such a scheme are mitigated.

HYBRID VISUAL PROGRAMMING IN LOGO

Another successful hybrid programming system is the Logo language for children. Logo has been learned by thousands of ordinary schoolchildren who use it to write programs to draw pictures and produce animation (see figure 5.1).[5] Logo is a simple but flexible programming language that offers variables, iteration, conditionals, and recursion. Procedures can be defined and then called from within other procedures. Logo is another example of a hybrid visual programming system in which graphical primitives are also the primitives of a textual language. For example, in Logo, primitives include **fw** (move pen forward), **bw** (move pen backward), **lt** (turn pen to the left), and **rt** (turn pen to the right).

In Logo, just as in spreadsheets, procedures are textual, and the graphics are used to make program state visible. Program state itself happens to be graphics in Logo, but the principle is the same as in spreadsheets. Users write procedures in the compact formalism of a textual language that understands graphical primitives. To work out a procedure, a user can try each statement, one at a time, in the main window, immediately seeing how the drawing changes as a result of the execution of the statement. Then when the user knows what he wants, he goes to the editor to write all the statements down in a procedure definition, which itself can then be called interactively from the main window.

Note that in Logo, procedures are not attached to graphical objects; they simply use the graphical primitives as the primitives of the textual language. Thus the distributed code problems of spreadsheets, object-oriented languages, and HyperCard are avoided. In Logo, the graphics are effective in part because they are used to instantly update the presentation of program state, as the user types commands. As with spreadsheets, it

```
Copyright (C) 1992 by Harvard Associates, Inc.

Welcome to Logo!

? textscreen
? (setprinter 139)
Printer HP DeskJet activated.
? LOAD "adhouse.lgo
Loading from file ADHOUSE.LGO
HOUSE1 defined
Result: TRUE
? LOAD "vari
Loading from file VARI.LGO
ASHAPE defined
Result: TRUE
? printout house1
TO HOUSE1
     FD 100 RT 90 FD 200 RT 90 FD 100 RT 90 FD 200 RT 90 FD 100 RT 22.5 FD 100 R
T 135 FD 100 LT 67.5 FD 124 LT 112.5 FD 100 RT 22.5 LT 90 FD 125 BK 125 RT 90 LT
 22.5 BK 100 RT 112.5 RT 90 FD 100 RT 90 FD 125 RT 90 FD 100 BK 100 LT 90 FD 50
RT 90 FD 50 RT 90 FD 25 RT 90 FD 50 LT 90 FD 25 FD 50 PU LT 90 FD 60 PD ASHAPE 2
0 4 HT
END

?
```

Figure 5.1
A Logo program written by Anthony Darrouzet-Nardi, age 11, for a drawing of a house, doing it the left-brained way

is not simply "graphicalness" that is important, but using graphics in a particular way, to immediately show program state.

HYBRID VISUAL PROGRAMMING IN CAD SYSTEMS

The designs produced by CAD systems are so obviously geometric objects that it might be supposed that some form of visual programming would be most suitable to CAD systems. But Tee (1992) found that CAD users who have access to textually-based "parametric design" tools prefer them to working directly with the geometry of the designs themselves.

In CAD, parametric design is the use of parameters and constraints to define the geometry of a feature or part. For example, Tee (1992) explains how to to define a square parametrically:

The constraints specified for the square include the perpendicular relationships at the corners as well as all four line segments being of equal length. [A] parameter, A, . . . drives the length of one side (hence driving the length of all sides of the square . . .). To create a square from this model, one specifies a numerical value for A. To make the square bigger, one changes the value of A to a larger number. (Tee, 1992)

Parametrics come in especially handy for modifying existing designs, which the users in Tee's (1992) study described as their most frequent activity. Fewer steps are required of the user because of the automation the parametrics provide. For example,

> [T]o move a hole feature in a solid, all a user would have to do [using parametrics] is change the value of the dimension locating the hole of a particular edge. This is considerably less cumbersome than having to manually move the geometrical components making up the hole, then changing the dimension associated with the location of the hole to the new value. (Tee, 1992)

Thus it is not surprising that in an experimental task, the users in Tee's study who were familiar with parametric methods "always attempted to make changes by modifying the value of parameters that drove positions, lengths, and shape" (Tee, 1992). The users who were not familiar with parametric methods "erase[d] and redr[ew] geometry that they want[ed] to change" (Tee, 1992).

However, there is a problem with parametric design: it is difficult to understand the constraints underlying a model. Changing the constraints, when that is necessary, is a difficult and dangerous task because changing one constraint can of course propagate changes to many (unknown) parts of the model. Design features may be constrained by more than one constraint, so the web of relationships can get quite complicated. Tee (1992) notes, "For example, a hole feature's location can be defined by its offset from two different edges, both of which are part of two different features." When a feature is to be deleted, undesirable side effects may result if its dependencies are not considered.

Tee (1992) suggests that the way to deal with the deficiency of parametrics is to provide good tools that allow users to visualize dependencies. At a minimum, a graph showing relations between features would be useful. As with spreadsheets, filtering, highlighting, and abstraction mechanisms would also help in the visualization process (Tee, 1992).

Thus, what we see in CAD systems is more the *potential* for hybrid visual programming than the actuality, at least in today's products. Tee (1992) suggests that parametric design, in which the user works in a textual mode, has great advantages in reducing the work needed to create a design but should be offered in a more supportive graphical environment. CAD, then, is another example of a system in which the most effective design is to combine text and graphics, using each where it best supports the task at hand.

VISUAL FORMALISMS AS APPLICATION FRAMEWORKS

What we have seen in spreadsheets is a hybrid programming environment in which a textual language is integrated into a visual framework that organizes and partially describes the computation. The basis of the spreadsheet is a table, but might there not be other such visual frameworks that could serve different applications? In a previous paper (Nardi and Zarmer, 1993), we argued that there are such frameworks, called *visual formalisms*, that include familiar graphic objects such as graphs, plots, panels, maps, and outlines as well as tables. These graphic objects are ubiquitous in the paper world because they provide so much help in organizing data. Once made into computer-based artifacts, their power expands many times over: now they are interactive objects that can be edited, searched, and browsed. New visual formalisms that are not derivative of familiar objects such as tables and graphs may also be developed; for example, Johnson and Shneiderman (1991) present treemaps, a means of visualizing hierarchical information structures. Visual formalisms are especially valuable because they can be specialized to support task-specific applications, as we describe below.

First, let's look generally at the concept of visual formalisms.

Visual formalisms are diagrammatic displays with well-defined semantics for expressing relations. In his article "On Visual Formalisms," David Harel (1988) stated:

The intricate nature of a variety of ... systems and situations can, and in our opinion should, be represented by *visual formalisms*: visual, because they are to be generated, comprehended, and communicated by humans; and formal, because they are to be manipulated, maintained, and analyzed by computers.

Visual formalisms are application frameworks. They provide a specific orienting framework in which to cast an entire application, just as the spreadsheet table does. An application framework is very different from a widget. A widget is a simple object whose purpose is to accept user commands or arguments, or to allow for the display and/or editing of simple data values. It exists not to organize whole applications but to give users access to small but significant pieces of an application. But many real-world applications (computer and noncomputer) are organized not around such simple forms as pushbuttons and menus, but around more complex visual displays that effectively organize and present relational information. For example, circuit design tools are often graphs, airplane cockpits are panels, and the patient records used in intensive care units are tables. A visual formalism is intended to help developers organize and present an entire complex application, or a significant piece of one. Visual formalisms are different in kind from widgets because they encode and visually reveal relational semantics. A widget is much more limited in scope; for example, a widget may show the value of a single variable or provide a means of issuing a single command. A visual formalism will, in most cases, be used in conjunction with widgets—for example, selectable nodes on a graph might reveal pop-up menus when selected. Several visual formalisms may be linked together to comprise a single large application.

Visual Formalisms in a Nutshell

Visual formalisms have several characteristics that make them good visual application frameworks.

- *Exploitation of human visual skills.* Visual formalisms are based on human visual abilities, such as detecting linear patterns or enclosure, that people perform almost effortlessly. Visual formalisms take advantage of our ability to perceive spatial relationships and to infer structure and meaning from those relationships (Cleveland, 1990). Visual formalisms are capable of showing a large quantity of data in a small space and of providing unambiguous semantic information about the relations among the data.

- *Manipulability.* Visual formalisms are not static displays but allow users to access and manipulate the displays and their contents in ways appropriate to the application in which they are used. Computer-based visual formalisms give us the ability to alter structure so that we can get, for example, a graph or table of just the configuration we want. Visual formalisms also permit visual manipulation through such means as filtering, symbolic scrolling, and iconifying (see figure 7.4 for an example of partition-based scrolling).

- *Specializability.* Visual formalisms provide basic objects that can be specialized to meet the needs of specific applications. They are at the right level of granularity—neither too specific nor too general. For example, graphs can be specialized to be schematics, petri nets, DAGs, semantic nets, and so forth.

- *Broad applicability.* Visual formalisms are useful because each expresses a fairly generic set of semantic relations, relevant to a wide range of application domains. Because a large number of applications can be designed around a given formalism, visual formalisms will eliminate a great deal of tedious low-level programming, as well as give developers ideas about editing and browsing techniques with which they may not be familiar, such as the use of fish-eye views for large datasets (Furnas, 1986; Ciccarelli and Nardi, 1988).

- *Familiarity.* Because the standard visual diagrams are so useful, they are found everywhere. Not only do they draw on innate perceptual abilities, but through constant exposure we become very familiar with them. Our schooling explicitly trains us in the use of the basic displays; for example, using calendars and learning matrix algebra provide experience with tables. Everyday activities provide opportunities to create and use visual formalisms, such as writing a shopping list or reading a map.

Are Visual Formalisms Really "Visual" or "Formal"?

It is necessary to ask what is "visual" and what is "formal" about visual formalisms. Their visualness derives from the fact that they impart information via visual cues such as space, color, texture, line, shape, movement—rather than through words. These cues are not necessarily pictorial in nature; an expanse of empty white space may be very visually expressive. The essence of visualness lies in exploiting *perceptual* rather than *linguistic* abilities. (See Larkin and Simon, 1987; Nygren et al., 1992. See also Raymond, 1991 for a discussion of the difference between notational and visual languages.)

We have avoided saying that visual formalisms are "nontextual" because written text has many visual cues that add to its semantic content: fonts, spacing, color, and capitalization all make a difference. Written text is a combination of visual and linguistic encoding. Nor are visual depictions always superior to text; it depends on the problem (see Green, Petre and Bellamy, 1991). Sometimes a few words are worth a thousand pictures. It should be noted that almost all visual representations use linguistic labels, so that rarely is an actual representation purely visual or purely linguistic. We nearly always explain figures and diagrams with captions (some quite lengthy) and attach labels and annotations.

Visual formalisms are formal in that, within an implementation, each visual formalism has a clear set of rules governing its editing and its form. For example, a table must maintain a rectangular shape, and an implementation should make it impossible to edit the table so that its rectangularity is not preserved (see Nardi and Zarmer, 1993, for a description of such an implementation). Visual formalisms can be formally represented for computational purposes; as Harel (1988) said, visual formalisms are formal in that "they are to be manipulated, maintained, and analyzed by computers." For those who find this use of the word "formal" unduly informal, we have sympathy; we chose the terminology to provide continuity and resonance with Harel's work, and because it suggests the computability of diagrams. Some may prefer the terminology "visual application frameworks."

Specializing Visual Formalisms

Although objects such as tables and graphs are clearly useful, they are much more useful when they can be specialized to meet the needs of a particular application. For example, Harel's (1988) statecharts, which formally describe a collection of sets and the relationships between them, combine graphs and Venn diagrams. Although Harel's work is quite new, Bear et al. (1989) have already created a specialization of statecharts, called objectcharts, for use in designing object-oriented software systems. And Heydon et al. (1989) specialized statecharts to model a language for specifying operating system security configurations. Using specializations of graphs and panels, Thomsen (1990) created an application for interacting with financial data. In the paper world, many worthwhile specializations of visual formalisms have been designed that would be much more powerful if computerized; for example, Cleveland (1985) describes specialized plots such as dot charts, sunflower plots, and brushed scatterplot matrices.

What exactly is the nature of the process of specializing a visual formalism? There are four elements: the ability to structurally edit the visual formalism; the ability to place application-specific content objects in the nodes of a visual formalism; the ability to add application-specific operations to the visual formalism; and the ability to use the visual formalism as a framework for application-specific programming languages. We look at each of these in turn.

A visual formalism must itself be editable, so that its structure can be changed to conform to the demands of an application; for example, a table may need spanning rows and columns of a particular width, or an outline a set of particular values for progressive levels of indentation, or a panel of horizontally or vertically aligned components.

The visual formalism must know how to contain and manage task- and domain-specific content objects; the visual formalism is not a drawing but an object-based representation in which nodes (e.g., cells in a table, nodes in a graph or outline) contain content objects, much as the cells of a spreadsheet hold numbers, formulas, and labels. While many applications can be modeled with simple integers and strings, it is the ability to put more specialized objects inside a visual formalism that provides more power for specialized applications. The content objects in a visual formalism are themselves full-fledged application objects with their own semantic operations; for example, transistors and resistors in a circuit design application, or innings and players in a baseball application, or patient records and treatment regimens in a clinical application. Content objects can even be other visual formalisms. An application might start, for example, with a panel on which components are placed, including perhaps a table or a graph or a plot.

Specializing some applications will require extending a visual formalism by adding new operations. A family tree editor, for example, would probably be implemented by extending a graph visual formalism. A basic graph visual formalism would provide only generic operations such as add- and remove-node, while a family tree editor should incorporate the additional semantics of genealogy, for example, an operation to "add descendant" and the constraint that you cannot be your own parent.

Visual formalisms provide a natural framework around which to build programming languages for establishing relations between objects in nodes. The exemplar here is the spreadsheet formula language, integrated with a table, as we have discussed. Designing programming languages that exploit structure can be done for other visual formalisms as well. Let's look more closely at extension languages for visual formalisms.

Extension Languages for Visual Formalisms

As we noted, supporting relations between content objects is an important part of what a visual formalism should do. Much of the power of spreadsheets inheres in the formula language that allows users to establish complex relations between elements in their models. The spreadsheet formula language understands the components of the spreadsheet table—cells and ranges of cells—and leverages that knowledge to make programming easier for users.

The coupling of the formula language and the table visual formalism has a couple of important advantages. First, it makes abstract concepts such as variable unnecessary. Users refer to data as *cells*—a concrete, graspable, viewable construct that seems to ease understanding (Nardi and Miller, 1990). Second, the formula language is able to provide an easy means of supplying program control: instead of writing iterative loops, users simply specify the range of cells over which to map an operation. In a conventional programming language, computing something equivalent to SUM(C1..C8) would require at least writing a loop iterating through elements of an array, and establishing and naming a loop counter and summation variable. In spreadsheets, iterative control is extremely easy; indeed, the user thinks not about "iterating" but about *summing* (or whatever the operation of interest is)—a meaningful task-specific concept of direct relevance to the user's work.

The question is: Can this coupling we observe in the spreadsheet formula language be applied to other visual formalisms? We think the answer is yes, that establishing relations between content objects in nodes in any visual formalism will be a useful capability. For example, in an organizational chart application, the user might want to refer to one branch of the organizational tree and ask the application to perform a headcount operation (e.g., find out how many people work for a particular manager). Just as in spreadsheets, this can be done by casting the problem in terms of visible, concrete nodes. Similarly, one can imagine operations for components of schematics and panels, regions of maps, points on plots, and so forth.

Visual formalisms support specialization in that you can edit a visual formalism's structure; put things inside it in an organized fashion; give it the operations that make sense for a particular application; and use it to give programming languages visible, concrete structures. Visual formalisms exhibit just enough structure of their own to provide a strong point of departure for application development, but not so much that they cannot be flexibly modified and extended to serve as frameworks for a wide variety of applications. The capacity for such specialization provides the kind of scope necessary for an object to serve as a true application framework.

SUMMARY

We have proposed that visual programming, as described in chapter 4, is not the only appropriate means of using visual techniques in end user programming environments. Another way is to create hybrid systems: visual application frameworks that articulate with textual programming languages. In this approach, a graphical format is used to display data, and to make the components of computation concrete structures that constitute, in part, the primitives of the textual language. In this way, text and graphics are both used to good advantage. Spreadsheets and the Logo language for children are examples of successful hybrid end user programming systems. CAD systems have the potential to support textually based parametric design, a definite advance in CAD, with graphical tools that show important aspects of program state.

To encourage the development of hybrid systems, reusable visual application frameworks should be available as a basis for designing and developing an end user system. Some familiar frameworks that are even more useful in their computerized form include tables, graphs, plots, panels, maps, and outlines. In chapter 7, a prototype system, ACE (Application Construction Environment), that supports the development of visual application frameworks is described.

6

Collaborative Work Practices

We must all hang together, or assuredly we shall all hang separately.
—Benjamin Franklin

Thus far our discussions have presupposed a single user for whom individual cognitive and motivational factors determine the appropriateness of a given software system. Now it is time to look at the larger system within which applications are created, to consider the *social matrix* in which people work, to see how social arrangements affect application development. This is important for two reasons: (1) so that we can understand how to change or introduce work practices that support end user computing, and (2) so that we can design software that supports and takes advantage of appropriate work practices. Our key argument is that by working collaboratively, end users can create richer, more sophisticated applications than they could working independently. Collaborative programming affords end users more power, but not at the expense of ease of use. We examine the structuring of spreadsheets and CAD systems to see how each system supports collaborative work practices. But first we look at the different kinds of cooperating users, in a variety of settings, to how they work together to create applications.

Recent studies reveal that an important aspect of end user computing is the emergence of *programming communities of cooperating users* that develop when a program is used by a group of people in some social setting such as an office or lab (Clement, 1990; Mackay, 1990a; MacLean et al., 1990; Nardi and Miller, 1991, Gantt and Nardi, 1992). We often envision a lonely end user laboring in isolation, just barely keeping the computer at bay at the best of times, and *mano a mano* with the machine at the worst of times. But these studies show that quite the opposite is true—end users make good use of other people in their social environments to help them solve their computing problems and to compensate for gaps in their own knowledge of computers.

The empirical studies, which span a wide range of computing arenas, show an unmistakable pattern of cooperative development of end user applications in which different kinds of users work together to produce an application (Clement, 1990; Mackay, 1990a; MacLean et al., 1990; Nardi and Miller, 1991, Gantt and Nardi, 1992). In our spreadsheet study we found that communities of users span a *continuum* of programming skill ranging from end users to local developers to programmers. *End users* have little or no programming education and tend not to like computers strictly for their own sake; they are very focused on their own domain interests. *Local developers* are domain experts who happen to have an intrinsic interest in computers and have more advanced knowledge of a particular program. They serve as a resource for end users, training them and writing code for them. *Programmers* are professionally trained. They contribute bits of code to the programs of end users and local developers and help them learn new things. Programmers have a much broader, deeper knowledge of computing than do local developers (e.g., knowledge of compilers, operating systems, languages, architectures, programming methodologies).

One of the most interesting aspects of cooperative computing among end users is the existence of local developers. In settings where a program is widely used, local developers seem to spontaneously emerge. In our spreadsheet study we discovered the presence of local developers in virtually all the settings we studied (Nardi and Miller, 1991). Local developers are domain experts—not professional programmers—who have a natural affinity for computers and develop deeper expertise in specific application programs such as spreadsheets. They tend to read manuals more frequently than ordinary end users do, they cultivate relationships with programmers and learn from them, and they exhibit "tinkering" behavior—playing around with programs above and beyond the call of duty.

For example, Jennifer noted the existence of a local developer in her office:

Interviewer: Okay, so other people around here know about spread-sheets. Are there particular people you go to, or, oh, I mean I'm trying to get a feel for how you kind of learn new things as you go along.

Jennifer: Oh, there is one other guy in my department in Account-ing/Finance that knows quite a bit about spreadsheets just by fiddling around with them. I think he stays here late at night and plays with them. Ha, ha!

Jennifer, a dyed-in-the-wool accountant, found it quite funny that some-one would stay late at night and "play with" spreadsheets. However, she used this local developer as the first line of defense in learning new spread-sheet features. She admitted avoiding manuals whenever possible.

Jennifer: ... I never really ever read a manual, not for Supercalc or Lotus. I just ask people.

Interviewer: You know other people have told me that, and I just find that amazing that people don't read manuals.

Jennifer: ... if I get [really] stuck, then I go look it up ...

Clement (1990), Mackay (1990a), and MacLean et al. (1990) found strikingly similar patterns of computing behavior in very different settings.

In a study of Project Athena users including secretaries, managers, pro-grammers, and other staff, Mackay (1990a) found widespread sharing of UNIX customization files.[1] She noted that, though we tend to think of customization as a private, personal matter, the dominant mode of setting up and modifying customization files in her study involved a great deal of social interaction; there were many exchanges of files, and much in-formation sharing among different kinds of users. Systems programmers tried out new things in customization files and made their files accessible to others via broadcast mechanisms. It was the "translators," as Mackay calls them, who offered direct help to less sophisticated users and aided them in tailoring their customization files to meet their personal needs. Translators, much like the local developers we found in the spreadsheet world, occupy an intermediate position on the technical sophistication ladder. They have good communication skills and provide an important bridge between less sophisticated end users and the advanced program capabilities developed by sophisticated programmers (such as those put out for broadcast by the Athena programmers), or facilities offered directly in a program. It is important to note that part of the effectiveness of translators derives from the fact that they are not outside consultants but are an integral part of an existing social network. They often bring a great deal of domain knowledge to the translating task, making it easier to get the functionality that the end user really wants. Mackay (1990a) recommended that we recognize and support the role of translator and provide tools that support translator activities.

Mackay's research shows how sharing in a programming community goes beyond the informal training exchanges described in earlier studies (e.g., Scharer, 1983; Lee, 1986; Nelson and Cheney, 1987) to include exchanges of code (e.g. making new customizations available by broadcast), and direct changes made to user files orchestrated by translators. We found the same code exchange and direct edits in the spreadsheet study (Nardi and Miller, 1991).

A third study that uncovered the important bridging function of the intermediaries who bring together end users and advanced programming techniques is MacLean et al.'s (1990) work at EuroPARC on tailorable office systems. MacLean and his colleagues classified three kinds of users according to programming sophistication: workers, "tinkerers" and programmers. In the office setting that was studied, tinkerers performed the same function as local developers and translators in helping less sophisticated users gain access to more advanced program features. MacLean et al. (1990) argued that though we should make tailoring mechanisms more accessible to everyone, it is also important to make tailoring a "community effort" that draws on the varied expertise of different kinds of users.

A systems consultant who we interviewed during the course of the spreadsheet study told a similar tale. Ralph Kimball described his experience of finding local developers whom he calls "advocate end users" in the world of Metaphor Capsule programming.[2]

Interviewer: ... [We've heard that customers have written a lot of Capsule applications actually collected by Metaphor and given to other customers.] ... Who wrote those capsules, and what were they?

Kimball: ... It didn't quite turn out that way, but it was close. The Capsules were written either by what I would call advocate end users, ... [the] ten percent of the end users who in fact like computers and choose to program, [or by professional support staff]. . . . That's a constant number of [advocate end users] of around 10–20 percent—10 percent in every department of any group. There are people who are prone to do this, and who will do complicated things, and who like programming. . . . I'd say, half of [the Capsule applications] are written by those kinds of people, and the other half are written by professional support staff . . .

Earlier in the interview Kimball had described the kinds of applications less sophisticated Capsule users build as he discussed demonstrating the Metaphor Capsule to prospective new users:

Kimball: . . . It was really easy to understand the simplest possible example [of what a Capsule can do]—query to spreadsheet to plot. I mean, that has been demoed a thousand times, at least, maybe ten thousand times. And it was just three icons. . . . The standard demo, you know, you did a query, then you manually transferred things to the spreadsheet, and you manually transferred it to a plot. You say, "What if I wanted to do that tomorrow?" and then you connected it with the arrow, and then you ran it. . . . That's a very powerful demo and captures the imagination of effectively anyone who watches it. It makes them think, "I can do this." And . . . I think most people at least try that, even if they're sort of non-programmers, they try sort of that level of stuff. In truth, right there is the limit of what 80 percent at least of the Metaphor end users ever do.

In terms of Metaphor Capsule programming, Kimball observed the same pattern found in the other studies: end users construct simple programs, "advocate end users" construct more advanced applications, and professional programmers create the complex applications that require more programming knowledge.

COLLABORATION AMONG SPREADSHEET USERS

In the spreadsheet study we found that collaboration among different kinds of users is the rule, not the exception, and that collaboration takes several forms (Nardi and Miller, 1991). Typically, end users do most of their work within the formula language, and they are aided by local developers or programmers when they need macros; sophisticated graphs and charts; custom presentation formats, such as a new format for displaying cell values; formulas with advanced spreadsheet functions such as date-time operations; and complex formulas, such as a formula with many levels of nested conditionals. Sometimes local developers or programmers create code (macros, etc.) that they give directly to end users; other times they help end users themselves learn how to do something new. Together with professional programmers (such as those working in MIS departments), local developers work with end users to create more sophisticated applications than the end user could create alone. We found that users also debug spreadsheets cooperatively; this may happen entirely within a set of end users working on a common application (Nardi and Miller, 1991).

COLLABORATION AMONG CAD USERS

As we have seen, in some settings no planned, managed infrastructural changes in work practices are required to support the emergence of programming communities, which spontaneously develop as an outgrowth of existing social networks. Code and knowledge are readily exchanged among those in a programming community in the course of everyday, informal relationships.

In our study of CAD use, however, we found that under some circumstances a somewhat different pattern evolves (Gantt and Nardi, 1992). We studied CAD use in seven companies, and in three of those companies we found the existence of "gardeners," that is local developers whose roles have been formalized such that they receive resources and recognition for their support activities (just as advocated by Mackay, 1990). (The other four companies had typical informal local developers.) The term *gardening* comes from the argot of one large corporation we studied where local developer roles have become formalized with the intent of "growing productivity." Gardeners are responsible for nurturing fellow employees and providing strong support so that employees can perform as effectively as possible. Gardeners are a special case of local developer; they are distinct from other local developers in that they are given recognition, time, and resources for pursuing local developer activities. Some gardeners are full-time, others part-time.

In addition to performing traditional local developer duties, gardeners are responsible for writing and disseminating standard CAD macros and programs at the corporate, division, or department level and for researching and providing new tools to end users. The macros and programs they write may originate from their own observations of what is needed, or they may be created in response to user requests for certain capabilities or requests from management. Sometimes a gardener sees a macro or program a user has written that looks useful for the whole group. The gardener takes the user's file, tests the code, modifies it if necessary, and then disseminates it to the group. Gardeners are always on the lookout for tools to enhance the group's productivity. The most advanced gardeners (and some local developers) also write shell scripts in UNIX, and write programs in the complex macro languages of some products. They may write programs in languages such as C or AutoLISP.[3] Such programming is required, for example, to perform calculations needed for CAD applications (e.g., calculating part placement) or to link a CAD application to other programs (for example, users might need enhanced plotting utilities or links to simulation or database programs) (see Gantt and Nardi, 1992). Gardeners also mediate between end users and systems administrators to help users with hardware and software configuration, maintenance, and upgrade.

Why does the formalization of the local developer role occur in the CAD world and not in settings such as offices using spreadsheets? This is a difficult question to answer, but our speculation is that it has to do with the large investment companies make in CAD software programs, which are quite expensive, as well as the high-end workstations on which CAD software often runs. In addition, CAD is often used in sophisticated networked computer systems connected to databases, simulation languages, varied output devices, and so forth, so there is a strong systems administration component to CAD use. Between the need for systems help and help with the CAD system itself, end users are looking for a good deal of support. As we discuss later, though the current impetus for gardening may be economic, we believe that a cost-effective gardening model is suitable for other environments and can support software use of many kinds.

COLLABORATIVE APPLICATION DEVELOPMENT AND SOFTWARE DESIGN

We have seen that programming communities emerge in organizations where groups of workers use a common software system. In particular these communities are marked by the emergence of local developers (or "translators" or "tinkerers" or "advocate end users"), a distinctive pattern common to varied settings when a program is used by a number of coworkers. We have also seen that local developers may evolve into the more formal role of gardener. Working cooperatively, end users create richer applications than they could if they were working alone. But what aspects of a software system itself support the emergence of a programming community?

The most obvious yet most critical answer is that the software system must have the advanced features that permit the more complex customizations and extensions enabled by local developers and programmers. If a spreadsheet contained only the formula language, and no macro language or graphing capabilities, end users would not enlist the support of local developers or programmers, and they would have simpler, less powerful applications. An instructive example to consider in this light was the decline of the first personal computer spreadsheet, VisiCalc, in the face of the more powerful Lotus 1-2-3. VisiCalc had no macro language and only a very primitive form of graphing. Lotus 1-2-3 had a macro language and good graphics. Though VisiCalc was introduced two years before 1-2-3, was priced about $300 cheaper, and enjoyed early success (selling many hundreds of thousands of copies (Levy, 1984)), it was driven out of the market by the superior capabilities of Lotus 1-2-3.

Thus, the foremost issue in designing software systems that support a community of users is that the system must incorporate the advanced features that make sophisticated customizations and extensions possible in the first place. But there is more to the story than that. The system should also be *modular*, keeping apart components that are primarily for the use of end users from those that can be learned and used separately by more advanced users. The modules can be thought of as being in layers, such that an end user may access a first layer that is easy to use and learn, while succeeding layers house modules for more advanced use. (The use of the terms "modules" and "layers" is largely metaphorical.) The important point about a module is that a user can approach it as a separable piece of functionality that can be learned and used independently of other aspects of a system.

A first-layer module in a system should be very high level, very task specific, and very easily learned. Other layers should permit more complex programming. Spreadsheets and CAD systems share this modular design. Spreadsheets have a basic layer—the formula language—*and* a macro language, which is much more flexible. By cleanly separating basic development tasks from more advanced functionality, the spreadsheet permits a distribution of tasks in which end users accomplish the basic implementation of a spreadsheet model, and those with more sophisticated programming knowledge provide smaller, more advanced contributions in the form of code and training. Likewise, many CAD systems are layered in offering basic drawing capabilities, a macro language for certain kinds of customization, and a more powerful language in which complex extensions can be accomplished, such as AutoLISP.

Having a modular software design in which different kinds of users use different modules is a way to resolve the problem of lack of power in task-specific programming languages. In chapter 3 we argued that a language that has a small number of simple task-specific operations is appropriate for end users because of the ease with which it can be learned and because of its direct support for users' problem-solving tasks. Such languages are necessarily going to lack the power and flexibility of a larger, more comprehensive language. This problem is resolved through cooperative work practices in which local developers and programmers write supplementary code for end users, using modules such as macro languages and extension languages like AutoLISP. What can make layered systems so effective for application development is not that end users finally "come up to speed" and learn advanced features but that, right from the start, they collaborate with more sophisticated users whose interests lead them to deeper study of a software system.

As we see from spreadsheet and CAD application development, end user systems do not have to employ a "single user" model; they can take advantage of the fact that different kinds of users work together to create applications. At the same time it must be remembered that end users must be able to do *the bulk of the application development* themselves; what makes collaboration among spreadsheet and CAD users work is that end users do *most* of the work (e.g., creating formulas in spreadsheets and drawings in CAD), and that local developers and programmers are adjuncts to the basic activity.

Some User Profiles
Cooperative computing only works because some users gain advanced expertise that they can then share with others. Thus it is critical that the

software provide advanced modules so that interested users can forge ahead and learn new things. At the same time, it must be recognized that some end users do not wish to learn advanced capabilities, and they will continue to rely on the expertise of local developers and programmers. We give brief profiles of two users from the spreadsheet study to illustrate the differing interests and motivations of two contrasting personalities. The first user, "Jeremy," has become a local developer. The second user, "Ray," has drawn a line in the sand for himself and prefers to work strictly within the formula language, obtaining macros from his customer support organization.

A conversation with Jeremy, a local developer, illustrates the quantum leaps in computing knowledge that an individual may experience. Jeremy described how he "discovered" macro programming. He is an executive—the chief financial officer of his company—and has never taken a computer science class. He received his MBA from Harvard Business School just prior to the time when quantitative methods (including mandatory instruction in the use of spreadsheets) were introduced into the curriculum.

We had been examining and discussing a macro program that Jeremy wrote. He explained that after reading the manual, it finally dawned on him how to do what he wanted to do. We were looking at one of his macros that selects files for printing and sets up printing parameters. The macro utilizes a counter, branching, and binary variables that can have 0 or 1 as values.

Jeremy: ... And then [the macro] compares [this variable] with the counter over here.

Interviewer: So this is real programming, basically.

Jeremy: Yes, right! ... It is exactly—a program. ... I found that out later. I didn't realize [that I was programming]. I thought I was being very clever—I was inventing something new!

Interviewer: But you were actually able to figure out how to do this by looking at examples in the manual?

Jeremy: That's right. Yeah, because I just mapped out: What is it that I want to do? ... What I would like to do is to have a series of instructions and have the macro search for those instructions, and based on certain yes/no conditions either perform the operation or go to the next step. That's really all I'm after. And so I kept on looking for [branching mechanisms], *and once I found them in the book I found so many different places where I could use them.* (emphasis added)

Although Jeremy would have liked to have had an easier time finding out about how to use conditionals in macros, once he found out, their generality opened up great new possibilities for his spreadsheets, and he was genuinely enthusiastic about "all the different places where I could use them." Not only did this new knowledge benefit Jeremy but his value in the programming community of which he is a part increased.

While individual end users may progress to learning new spreadsheet features, some users take advantage of certain advanced spreadsheet features *only through collaborations with more sophisticated users.* For example, many end users never learn to use macros, but they ask local developers or programmers to create macros that they then add to their programs. Some users draw a firm line for themselves even when they do know how to use a particular feature. Ray was telling us about a Lotus course on macros that he had taken, though he doesn't write many macros. Earlier in the interview he had mentioned that he has programmers in Customer Support write his custom menus:

Ray: I think the only Lotus course I took was last year, I took an advanced class, to learn how to do some fancy macros and some custom menus and so forth.

Interviewer: Was it useful?

Ray: On the macro side, yeah. It was. I learned some nifty little tricks—how to make your macros a little more standard, a little more useful. I haven't done any custom menus [which also require macros].

Interviewer: You have your people down in Customer Support do that stuff. Is that because it would take you too long to do it? It's not really the kind of thing that, er ... ?

Ray: Yeah. There really isn't a real need ... It's not my specialty. Most of what I do is ad hoc stuff.

Ray's point is that writing macros is not his real work. The programming effort is too great to justify taking his time away from "the ad hoc stuff," by which he means building forecasts and projections of budget activity in the departments he serves. *That* is his "specialty," not programming.

Users thus take advantage of advanced spreadsheet features such as macros without necessarily creating them themselves. Likewise, advanced spreadsheet functions such as database, date-time, and error trapping functions can be learned on an as-needed basis (often through interaction with more experienced users) or turned over to more advanced users to program. Graphs, charts, and many features of the user interface toolkit in spreadsheets provide further functionality that is often incorporated into end users' spreadsheets via cooperative computing practices. In having different, modular pieces of functionality that can be learned and used separately, spreadsheets allow different kinds of users to make distinctive contributions to a given spreadsheet application. Most importantly, the advanced expertise gained by individual users becomes more than just the knowledge of a single individual; it is a shared community resource.

A final point to be made about the importance of a layered software design is that such a design provides a growth path for individual users, even if they are not classic local developer types. Any individual user may learn and use the different pieces of a spreadsheet program at different points in his development of spreadsheet expertise. Progress along the path may take place at a very slow pace, but progress is possible.

Jennifer, for example, has been slowly building up her knowledge of spreadsheets for about five years. As we saw above, she lacks the interest to tinker around with spreadsheets, but still, she has been learning new things over time. She herself can help other less experienced users in her environment:

Jennifer: ... I [help] the Controller. When he's got something on his spreadsheet and he wants me graph it, I will say, "Can I borrow your disk?" and I will just copy that.

Interviewer: Why doesn't he graph it himself?

Jennifer: He may not have time. Usually he doesn't have time. We are all teaching each other too. He usually comes to me, "Now how do I do this? I know you did this, [so show me]." So he doesn't read the book either!

Organizing software functionality around different kinds of cooperating users makes the range of things end users can do with software products much greater. It also acknowledges that some end users will eventually attain more expertise with a program as they become more familiar with it (whether they come to act in the supporting role of local developer or not) and will want to be able to learn more sophisticated capabilities. Some approaches to end user computing, such as programming by example or user modeling (Wolz, 1990), assume that not only do end users remain rather deficient but that they work in isolation, without a community of cooperating users. This is a limited view of end users and will ultimately mean inhibiting their growth and the kinds of applications they can create. In the CAD study, three of our users spontaneously brought this point up in their interviews. (We did not ask about it; it was a topic they introduced because they thought we would be interested.) "Rick" described three levels of users who should be supported—in his terms: "the idiot level, the full-fledged program level, and the power user level." "Warren," whose CAD system (for electrical engineering) offers few facilities for specialization, expressed dismay at the limitations of his system compared with another more sophisticated system some of his colleagues in another department were using:

Warren: I'm very jealous because they have this incredible flexible ability to change and do anything. One of the problems with people who write tools is that they assume ... they try to protect the users too much. And they don't recognize that there's different levels of users. You can have beginners, general users, and experts, and for the expert user, a lot of places will hire somebody to be an expert user just to [do] the customization, to do all the neat productivity things that make such a difference. *But you have to have that flexibility to start with.* ... I find myself with most of the PC [printed circuit] tools, there's not much I can do with them (emphasis added).

CULTIVATING GARDENERS

Just as software design should anticipate and plan for the existence of a community of cooperating users, work practices should be designed to optimize the differing contributions of the users in a programming community. The informal arrangements by which local developers support end users seem to be reasonably effective in enhancing the application development process. However, we believe that the gardening model is a better one because it ensures a reliable source of high-quality support. Cost-effective means of supplying gardening to a group can be achieved simply by using part-time gardeners where that is appropriate.

Let's look in more detail at the costs and benefits of gardening.

Our study of CAD use supports Mackay's (1990a) contention that the activities of local developers should be recognized and promoted. In the organizations that we studied in which the role of gardener has become a formal position, our assessment is that the benefits far outweigh the costs. End users are comfortable with CAD software because they are assured assistance in all aspects of CAD use – whether they are writing macros, learning new tools, or keeping abreast of the latest developments in CAD. Gardeners—who enjoy tinkering with computers—are given official leave to do so. Their communication talents are engaged as they provide an important bridge between system administrators on the one side and domain experts on the other, as well as communicating with users as they help them in debugging, learning new capabilities, and so forth. A gardener can save time and money by making it unnecessary for users to spend their time reinventing the wheel (creating redundant macros and programs); instead, the gardener offers standard versions of these resources to the entire group. Employees can be more productive because they are concentrating on their domain-related tasks. Establishing a gardener creates a finer-grained division of labor among software users that increases efficiency and motivation because it is firmly grounded in users' interests and abilities.

An important benefit of gardening is that managers can feel confident that the standardization and integrity of the macros, programs, and data used by their staffs will be maintained. Many managers and MIS personnel are made somewhat nervous by the whole notion of end user computing because the potential for chaos is real: data can disappear, users may waste time managing their systems instead of doing their work, and esoteric, personalistic specialization can reduce the utility of the programs developed by end users (see Panko, 1988). With a gardener in place, these concerns can be dealt with. It is the gardener's job to maintain standards and to offer users standard programs that they can use to get their work done. A gardener is someone between management and users and is trusted by both. Because gardeners are fellow domain experts and not outsiders who lack understanding of the everyday patterns of work and group interaction, they are more likely to be effective in dealing with the group's concerns. They can in fact anticipate these concerns and handle them proactively in a way that is impossible for outsiders such as systems analysts or MIS personnel.

A problem that we found with formalizing the local developer role is that not all managers recognize the benefits of having a "productivity" person on board. They may feel that this is a waste of a person who could be working to "contribute to the product." When a higher level of management mandates a gardener, the lower-level manager may feel that he or she is less effective and cannot utilize available resources in the best possible way (see Brooks and Wells, 1989). When this happens, at a minimum it would seem useful for managers to evaluate whether a project really does have enough resources. It may be that a manager has not thought through the benefits of including a productivity person in the group, or there may truly be a situation of insufficient resources. Adding a gardener to a group will involve some kind of economic analysis to determine just when the shifting of resources really makes sense. An indication of the need for a gardener is the situation in which a local developer is devoting considerable time to group support activities without official recognition and resources. From an economic viewpoint, adding a gardener to a group is not simply a matter of dividing up the same resources differently; there are true economies of scale in having a single person develop group macros, research new tools, and create common standards that allow a group to avoid the costly conflicts and obstacles that arise when group members are doing things differently. In some cases, certain kinds of productivity gains would not occur at all without a gardener; for example, a gardener may discover and bring to the group a new productivity tool that would not have been found by the average user trying to just get her work done. Experimentation with the gardener role will undoubtedly be necessary to make it fit the needs of the individual group. Some groups may feel the need for a full-time gardener, while others can get along with a part-time person.

Another problem with gardening is that there is not always a person with the right combination of technical and social skills available to assume the job. A person who is technically skilled but uninterested in intensive interpersonal interaction may not have much of a green thumb when it comes to helping other users. By the same token, a person without sufficient technical skill would not be an effective gardener. In our study we found a somewhat reluctant local developer, "Steve," who typifies at least part of the problem of finding the right mix of skills. Steve is a highly skilled electrical engineer. He and another engineer work on a project where they are creating complex simulations. Some of the other teams within the company are doing similar simulations, and, instead of learning how to program the simulation themselves, they ask Steve and his partner to help them. Steve's ambivalence about acting in a support role comes through in the following only half-humorous exchange:

Interviewer: So you guys are sort of the experts?

Steve: We're supposed to be, but . . .

Interviewer: (laughing) But you're not really? Well, do people come and ask you for help?

Steve: (laughing) Well, the thing is, I'm no smarter than any of those guys and . . . we try not to answer their questions.

Interviewer: So you don't like to share what you've done?

Steve: No, no, we will help. It depends on the time . . .

How do organizations cultivate gardeners? The right mix of skills is important, as the above example illustrates. A gardener cannot be randomly chosen out of a group of users; there must be genuine interest and enjoyment in assisting less knowledgeable users on the one hand, and the desire to learn one's way around the operating system and a programming language on the other hand. Brooks and Wells (1989) noted that when users are learning a new system in a training class, often one person stands out in interest and ability and can be identified fairly early as a potential local expert. More generally speaking, their point is well taken: rather than selecting someone to be a gardener at the introduction of a new system, it is better to wait until users have had some exposure to the system, looking for those who gravitate naturally toward its use.

The results of our study indicate that another factor that contributes to gardeners' effectiveness is that they come from the rank and file: they know the domain, the users, the frustrations, and problems. The need to expend great effort translating domain knowledge to computer experts is avoided. Gardeners who are domain experts have "been there before"—

and they show concern and empathy for their users. They know how it feels to be frustrated and unproductive because of software or hardware limitations.

A problem that Mackay (1990a) reported in her study of UNIX customization was that the local developers (or translators as she called them) often were not as knowledgeable about computers as would have been desirable, and as a result, they sometimes distributed buggy code throughout the organization. We did not find this to be a problem among the gardeners we studied because their level of computer expertise was high, and they were able to meet the technical challenges. While CAD users may typically start out with an advantage in having a good technical background, users in other fields can strive to attain a high level of computer competence through training and studying on their own. (Indeed, many of our CAD users had taken programming and product classes and had devoted a great deal of time to self-study.) Cultivating gardeners should involve making the time and money available for such training and study. More generally, solving the problem of distributing quality code means supporting the local developer role in a formal way, to ensure that adequate time is devoted to testing and debugging code to be given out to the group.

If an organization can manage to train gardeners to a high enough standard, the need for professional programmers largely disappears, at least with respect to the well-designed commercially available products that support end user computing, such as CAD systems. In our study we found no instance of users resorting to programmers for assistance in specializing their CAD software. When macros and programs are written by gardeners, it is with group use in mind (so idiosyncratic code is not produced) and with a good command of the domain and the end users' concerns. In Mackay's (1990a) study, the UNIX customizations were written by professional programmers for their own use, and the "translating" needed before end users could make use of the customizations was considerable.[4] Of course that was a different setting, and the comparison cannot be stretched too far, but the point is that gardeners can produce code from the outset that is intended for group use, and, most importantly, with a very clear picture in mind of the group's needs and preferences.

While we believe that a major strength of gardeners is their origin as domain experts, we can also see a potential problem in this arrangement. Over time, full-time gardeners may lose touch with the domain side of gardening as their activities come to be defined purely in terms of support. The most effective gardeners will make a special effort to keep up with advances in their field and to be cognizant of the changing work practices in which they themselves are not directly participating. Some gardeners may want to rotate out of gardening periodically to renew and update their domain knowledge.

REMOTE COLLABORATION AND SOFTWARE REUSE

In this chapter we have concentrated on communities of cooperating users, and how to design software systems and work practices that support collaboration. But there is another aspect of cooperation that is less direct, but equally important: the sharing of software artifacts.

Tee (1992) reported that the CAD users in her study rarely started a design from scratch, but worked from existing designs, often designs created by someone else. Even a design for a completely new part is typically based on existing parts. Thus much sharing of drawings goes on between users, some of whom may never have met each other. Tee (1992) notes that this situation means that "it is important for drawings to be communicable and well-documented," once again underscoring the need for good visualizations of the constraints underlying parametrically designed parts. Annotation facilities to document part design are also important to maximize the effectiveness of reuse (Tee, 1992).

In the spreadsheet study we found a very similar situation. Users share spreadsheets in the form of templates, and often the assumptions underlying a template are unclear and must be communicated to the person attempting to use the template. For example, the user might need to know whether a particular cell value is based on headcount or revenue. Documentation facilities that allow users to make such annotations in a clearly communicated way would be helpful. Users in our study reported that currently available facilities that allow notes to be attached "behind" cell values are inadequate, and a new format that makes annotations more visible and flexibly organized would be desirable. As in CAD systems, users also need better visualization facilities for exposing cell dependencies. The cooperative debugging practices we described for spreadsheet users would also be better supported by visualization and documentation facilities (Nardi and Miller, 1991).

Considerations of software reuse amplify the need for the visualization and annotation facilities that are necessary to support the activity of individual end users. The sharing implicit in reuse also dictates that end user systems adequately provide system-level capabilities for versioning, permissions, and updates to manage the inevitable difficulties of multiperson systems (see Berlin and O'Day, 1990).

SUMMARY

Collaborative programming involves both remote collaborations achieved via reuse of software artifacts and face-to-face or media-supported communication in which users directly communicate problems and solutions to one another. End user systems should take advantage of the information sharing that collaboration affords and the immense opportunities it presents to end users to create more sophisticated applications.

The division of labor is a cultural universal—every society, even the simplest thirty-person band of hunter-gatherers, has its specialists. No one is expected to know how to do everything—or to be interested in knowing how to do everything. For our purposes, the problems are to establish a division of labor that promotes end user programming and to design both software systems and work practices that take advantage of that division of labor.

Making software systems too simple means that the kinds of applications end users will be able to create will be limited. Software systems should be designed to take advantage of the naturally occurring division of labor in which end users do the bulk of the application development but are aided at critical junctures by more computationally sophisticated users. Software systems that do not incorporate more sophisticated modules such as macro languages or extension languages miss an opportunity to provide a richer environment for end users who can take advantage of advanced program features through cooperative computing practices.

As we have seen from the examples of programming communities in a variety of programming arenas, what gives local developers their *raison d'etre* and incorporates programmers into the community inhabited by end users is the possibility of relatively more advanced users aiding relatively less advanced users through their superior knowledge of advanced program features. Rather than have a system that is limited to things that are easy enough to provide purely through simple interaction techniques such as setting variables in forms, the alternative is to have programs that layer complexity such that end users can accomplish many but not all programming tasks, turning to more experienced users to obtain either training or code when their lack of programming knowledge prevents the successful completion of a task. Organizing programming functionality around different kinds of cooperating users makes the range of things end users can do with computers much greater.

Just as software design should incorporate the notion of communities of cooperating users, those communities themselves can be better organized and managed. Experience with CAD systems has given us a model in which local developers evolve into gardeners who nurture end users' productivity by providing a high level of software support. Being domain experts themselves gives gardeners a significant edge over more traditional forms of support such as customer hotlines or in-house systems administration support. Gardening is effective because it establishes a division of labor based on people's skills, interests, and abilities. Most important, gardeners provide a reliable source of high-quality support to users working with complex software systems. One of the informants in our study, a "head gardener" who coordinates the activities of a worldwide network of gardeners, summed up the value of gardening this way:

There's an analogy [to gardening] that I think is very good. You know, [here at our company] we have these wonderful hardware systems . . . and we have this wonderful software that we're all using. But we're not really using it to its full potential . . . I'd say that even though we're doing all this great stuff, we're using maybe about 50, 60, 70 percent of the capacity that these tools have to offer. And it's kind of like having this race car in the Indy 500. You know, your boss is giving you this wonderful, fast, fast car, but . . . we don't have a pit crew to help us gas up the car, and fine tune it, and get it to run really fast and beat everybody else. So it's really kind of the development engineer's out there racing this car, trying to win this race; getting out of the car, gassing it up, changing the tires themselves, and trying to understand all about this car. We don't have a team in place to help people do this. We just have a bunch of individuals. And I'm trying to build these teams so that we can help each other out more.

The image of team building is an appealing one and makes good organizational sense. More effective use of software systems will be made when managers cultivate gardeners, and when software design efforts take into account the patterns of cooperation among different kinds of users working together to create applications.

7

Scenarios of End User Programming

"Oh Kitty, how nice it would be if we could only get through into Looking Glass House! I'm sure it's got, oh! such beautiful things in it! Let's pretend there's a way of getting through into it, somehow, Kitty. Let's pretend the glass has got all soft like gauze, so that we can get through. Why, it's turning to a mist now, I declare! It'll be easy enough to get through ..."
—Alice to Kitty in *Through the Looking Glass* by Lewis Carroll

Offices, factories, corporations, government agencies, schools, universities, hospitals, laboratories, and libraries will continue to need complex software systems to make the functioning of these institutions more manageable, to promote creative work, to enhance instruction, and to make workers more productive. To use computers cost-effectively, people within the organizations will have to develop applications because professional programmers are too expensive and too scarce. The process of transferring domain knowledge to a programmer, and going through the necessary iterations to get the desired application, is inefficient. Post hoc extension and customization of an application involves the same cycle of inefficient use of human resources if programmers must be involved, but the need for such extension and customization is the rule rather than the exception. End users who themselves have control over computational resources will be able to effectively manage application development and ongoing extension to meet changing needs. Computing work must therefore be distributed across the people in an organization, not bottlenecked at programming professionals. One piece of the solution to the productivity puzzle then, is to increase the value of computers by increasing the efficiency and effectiveness with which ordinary people use computers to build the applications they need.

As we have seen, most research efforts in the realm of end user programming have aimed at one of two targets: inventing a new interaction technique to relieve users' problems with communicating with the machine or discovering how to make conventional languages work for end users. A different way to look at the problem of end user programming is from a semantic vantage point, focusing on users' tasks. In this approach, the overriding goal is to leverage users' skills and interests in the design of a programming system.

The task-specific approach adopts a positive rather than negative view of end users: instead of emphasizing users' deficiencies to be remedied, the task-specific approach attempts to capitalize on users' strengths. The idea is to build on users' existing domain knowledge and skills; end users have spent years building up a corpus of domain expertise and communication ability that can be successfully exploited in end user programming systems. We hope to see an end to the use of such words as "casual," "novice," "naive," or "nonprogrammer" with respect to end users—end users are serious professionals with extensive training, experience, and knowledge in their chosen field. Computer-centric terms such as "novice" obscure the possibilities for creating appropriate end user systems and are prejudicial in assigning prominence to the computer.

In a less philosophical vein, we believe that end user systems should be task-specific because users do not want to learn or use unfamiliar low-level programming primitives and they prefer to work within the idiom of their domain tasks. For these reasons, conventional languages are to be rejected as a solution to the problems of end user programming. An understanding of the tasks users perform will dictate the specific interaction techniques that are useful, but a specific interaction technique is not the point of departure for system design.

It is noteworthy that virtually all of the successful end user systems in widespread use today are task-specific: spreadsheets, statistical packages, CAD systems, 4GLs, text formatters that allow significant customization such as FrameMaker, and systems such as Mathematica and Logo. Some system genres are highly specialized. CAD systems, for example, are specialized for particular domains such as architecture, and electrical, mechanical, and civil engineering. Document systems may be specialized for the production of different types of documents such as slides, legal documents, and business forms. None of these systems is perfect; they all have easily enumerated flaws. But it is impossible not to be struck by the twin facts that these systems are in use by millions of actual end users, and the one thing they all share is task-specificity.

The interaction techniques used in these systems vary widely. Some are hybrid systems that incorporate both text and graphics, such as spreadsheets with a textual formula language and a graphical display of program state in the spreadsheet table, or CAD systems with textual macro languages coupled with graphical drawing capabilities. Others are purely textual such as 4GLs and statistical packages (especially the earlier versions of these packages, which have been successfully used since the 1970s). Text formatting systems often make use of a forms-based interface. We do not know of a task-specific visual programming system in widespread use, except possibly HP VEE (whose base of active users we cannot estimate). Programming by example is a new technique that has not yet had time to percolate to commercial use; its future will be interesting to watch.

The importance of task-specificity in end user systems suggests that the problem of helping end users to be more productive with computers does not lie in extensive education, or in providing scripting languages that are general-purpose but "easy" to use, or in finding the ultimate interaction technique. Rather, designers should start with a clear sense of and respect for the tasks that end users will be doing, and then design a system that best supports those tasks.

But we can say more than this. Based on our ethnographic studies of spreadsheet and CAD users, as well as our reading of the literature on end user programming, we have argued that a recipe for successful end user programming systems includes task specific programming languages, visual application frameworks, and support for collaborative computing practices. End user computing environments should support a specific set of activities for a community of cooperating users who will fall within some continuum of interest and skill with computers. This implies a large number of specialized computing environments. In order to develop the task-specific environments for the many domains that are not yet served by commercial products, good software tools will be necessary, if development is to be cost-effective. Several such tools are at the research stage and promise to make the development of highly specialized end user programming environments cheaper and faster. These tools include ACE (Johnson, 1992; Zarmer and Chew, 1992; Zarmer et al., 1992; Johnson et al., 1993;

Nardi and Zarmer, 1993), BOZ (Casner, 1991), ITS (Gould, Boies and Lewis, 1991), Garnet (Myers et al., 1990), Unidraw (Vlissides and Linton, 1990), Andrew (ITC, 1988), D2M2-Edit (de Baar, Foley and Mullet, 1992), Workspaces (Olsen, McNeill and Michell, 1992), Spark (Marques et al., 1992), Mosaic (Parker, 1992), and Humanoid (Szekeley, Luo and Neches, 1992). These systems attempt to provide higher level software building blocks, above general programming languages and windowing toolkits, that facilitate the development of the semantic and/or user interface components of applications.

One such effort is ACE (Application Construction Environment), a prototype system built at Hewlett-Packard Laboratories in Palo Alto. ACE is a set of C++ class libraries and includes *ACEKit*, a user interface management system to handle the wiring of user operations to the user interface (Zarmer, 1991); *ACE Visual Formalisms*, a collection of visual formalisms to serve as visual application frameworks, including tables, graphs, panels, and outlines (Nardi and Zarmer, 1993); *GLUE* (Generalized Language for User Extension), an extension language linked to visual formalisms for the creation of task-specific languages (Zarmer et al., 1992; Zarmer and Chew, 1992) and *Selectors*, a set of "smart" widgets (Johnson, 1992). See figure 7.1 for a diagrammatic overview of ACE.

A particularly important aspect of ACE is the extension language that exploits the structure of visual formalisms and allows for the creation of task-specific languages directly linked to a visual form. In ACE, the extension language understands nodes in any visual formalism and can reference them and their contents. It is interpretive so that it can be used to write languages that behave much like the spreadsheet formula language; changes in one node are propagated to other nodes and are immediately displayed within the visual formalism. The extension language is the *basis for* task-specific languages for particular applications; programmers write primitives (such as SUM) using the mechanisms provided by the extension language. The extension language will enable programmers to develop useful languages that take advantage of the structure and appearance of visual formalisms, just as the spreadsheet formula language does.

The details of the software components in ACE are described in the publications cited; in this chapter we sketch two applications that use ACE components to show how such an application construction toolkit can make it easier to create highly task-specific end user programming

ACE

Application Construction Environment

Goals:
Produce specialized, task-specific applications
Enable end user programming

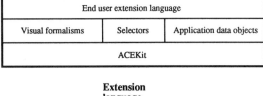

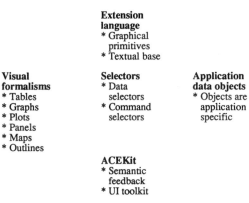

Figure 7.1
ACE overview

environments. These examples are intended to suggest how future end user programming systems can be designed and constructed.

CREATING A HOSPITAL FLOW SHEET

Our first example highlights the use of visual formalisms and sketches a scenario of collaborative development. We describe the process of building an application similar to an existing, commercially available Hewlett-Packard product, CareVue.[1] CareVue is an automated patient record based on the tabular flow sheet used in hospital intensive care units to record patient data. Each row in the flow sheet represents a different measurement, and each column represents the time a measurement was taken.

To build CareVue, we start with a table visual formalism. The basic exercise is to specialize the table and its content objects (see chapter 5)

File Cell Section Edit Layout Partition Lock Debug								

Selected Cell: (0, 0)   type: String | Reset | OK | Vitals|

	0	1	2	3	4	5	6	7
0	Vitals							
1								
2								
3								
4								
5								
6								
7								
8								
9								
10								

Change cell contents to a new object of a specified type

Figure 7.2
Creating the CareVue application. We begin building the application by asking
for a table of 10 x 20 cells. We make the content type of each cell a string, as a
beginning default. This is done through a menu selection from the *Cell* menu at
the top of the table. We put in some text labels by typing directly into the cells. In
this first step, we have selected the table as a visual/semantic framework within
which to construct our application. We have thought about cell content types,
and sketched a little application data into a cell as a text label.

until we have achieved a hospital flow sheet that captures our intended
domain semantics. Specializations will include altering the structure of
the table, placing appropriate content objects into table cells, and adding
selectors to access end user operations.

Figures 7.2 through 7.4 illustrate the interactive process of rearranging
the table and selecting cell content objects that create CareVue. The basic
activities of application building are to alter the layout of the table so that
it organizes the application data properly and to place the correct content
objects in cells.

As you study figures 7.2 through 7.4, notice that the structural alter-
ation of the table and the basic layout of the information in cells can
easily be managed by an end user; no programming knowledge is required. The entire flow sheet can be laid out using text labels so that
its overall design can be established by an end user. Programmer-created

File Cell Section Edit Layout Partition Lock Debug

Selected Cell: (1, 7)　　　type: String　　　[Reset]　[OK]

	0	1	2	3	4	5	6
0			Hewlett-Packard CareVuwe				
1	Patient:		John Smith				
2	Date:		January 1, 1991				January 2,
3	Time:		8am	12pm	4pm	8pm	8am
4	Vitals	HR					
5		ABP Sys/Dias					
6		MAP					
7		Resp Rate					
8							
9							
10							

Split a cell evenly based on number of columns spanned

Figure 7.3
Specializing the CareVue table. Using the mouse, we join some cells to create
spanning cells for headers *Patient, Date, Time* and the daily time periods that the
flow sheet tracks. We type the headers directly into the spanning cells as text labels.
Using the mouse, we drag out the second column to a larger size to accomodate the
larger labels needed for *HR, ABP Sys/Dias*, etc. We now have the basic format of a
flow sheet. In this step we have structurally altered the table to better organize the
patient data as used by doctors and nurses, and we have named the appropriate
categories in the headers. We type in some sample application data (*John Smith,
January 1991*) just to see how it looks.

application-specific objects can then be placed in the table later simply by
changing the content type of the relevant cells (see figure 7.4).

A programmer will have to be called in to make some extensions to the
ACE table visual formalism, and to create some application-specific objects. The major extension to the table visual formalism for the CareVue
application is to add coordination with a database in order to provide the
high data reliability required for a hospital application. CareVue allows
users to record annotations with data values. To support annotation, the
programmer constructs a specialized version of table cell objects that
provides for annotation objects as well as a primary data object. The cell
presenter objects would then be similarly specialized to indicate whether
an annotation was present and show it on demand. Cell objects can also

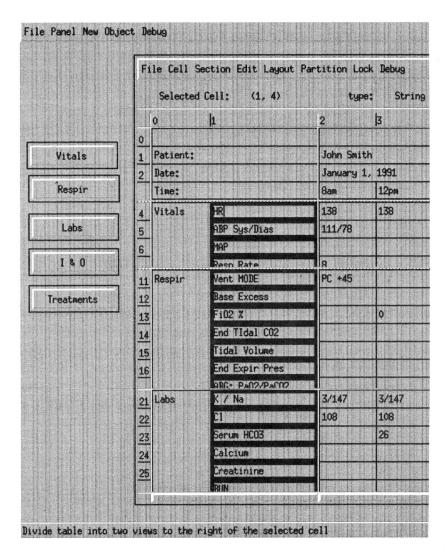

Figure 7.4
Completing the CareVue application. We join some more cells to create spanning cells for headers *Vitals, Respir, Labs*. We fill in the categories for *Respir* (*Vent MODE, Base Excess*, etc.) and *Labs* (*K/ Na, Cl*, etc.) that are needed. We decide that the subparts of the table *Vitals, Respir*, and *Labs* should be individually scrollable because each contains many subcategories, so we create them as partitions using the *Partition* menu at the top of the table. Now the flow sheet still shows the high-level categories *Vitals, Respir*, and *Labs* in a single screen, but the user can easily navigate further down within each category without losing the overall visual shape of the flow sheet.

We change some cell content types such as HR (heart rate) and Resp Rate to integer, and change ABP Sys/Dias (blood pressure) to the application-defined type

Reset | OK | HR

| 4 | 5 | 6 | 7 | 8 | 9 |

Hewlett-Packard Carevue

January 2, 1991

4pm	8pm	8am	12pm	4pm	8am
138	133	100		100	
100/80		90/70		95/71	
R		R		R	
AC		CNTL	CNTL	CNTL	
0				0	
3/147					
108					
				26	

"Blood Pressure." In this step we have again structurally altered the table to organize our application. We have modified the cell content types to more precisely capture application semantics, and we completed the categorization of patient data. The flow sheet will now accept three different kinds of data, any of which can be typed directly into the cells (data of an incorrect type are not accepted); the flow sheet has three individually scrollable partitions to support quick browsing; and it has all the other capabilities of ACE tables such as filtering and copying, should the need arise to use them. Each partition can be hidden to leave more room for the others. To finish the application, we place it inside a panel, and add Selector pushbuttons to select partitions.

be specialized to create intermediate values when they do not have a reported value.

A number of specialized data types are created by a programmer to represent values such as blood pressure. Integers could be used, but it is better to produce a class that models blood pressure more precisely (e.g., a blood pressure has two components; reasonable values are between 0 and 300; and one value should be lower than the other). This also allows for specialized presenters to show the values.

The visual appearance of CareVue is largely tabular, but it provides extra filtering and scrolling options to allow different predefined subsets of the table to be viewed at the press of a button (see figure 7.4). The ACE table visual formalism already provides the necessary filtering and scrolling services.

The last step in creating CareVue can be done by the end user: to produce the finished application, the table is placed on an ACE panel along with the ACE selectors that allow for the selection of table partitions (figure 7.4).

One of the motives for presenting the CareVue example in detail is to suggest how using visual formalisms as application frameworks changes the process of application development. The chief point is that application development merges with user interface design: one does not build "the application" and then tack on a user interface; rather, the two processes are more closely interwoven, and the user interface, by being subsumed in the application development process, comes to be a critical aspect of organizing and presenting application semantics—not an afterthought. Architecturally, ACE content objects are kept separate from visual formalism objects (see Nardi and Zarmer, 1993), but in terms of using these objects once application development begins, there is a much more commingled process. The visual formalism provides an overarching application framework that structures and displays application objects, exposing their individual values as well as their relations, rather than a more superficially conceived "view" of the objects.

Does using visual formalisms as the basis of application development mean that there is only one true visual formalism per application? Of course not; there are often multiple ways to display data that make sense. However, for *constructing applications*, including the necessary programming to create the application, it makes sense to provide a common, uni-

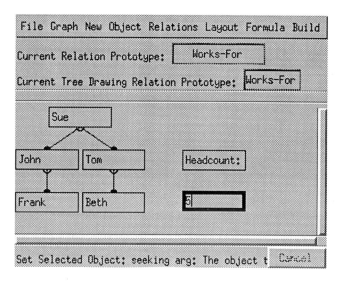

Figure 7.5
Creating an org chart

form application framework that is shared by a group of users and permits the development of an appropriate language that takes advantage of the structural components of the visual formalism, as do spreadsheets (see Nardi and Miller, 1990). In spreadsheets, users may do such things as plot data from the spreadsheet table (into line or bar charts, for example), but the table visual formalism remains the *application construction environment*.

CREATING AN ORGANIZATION CHART

Let's look at an application that uses a different visual formalism but follows the same principles we saw in CareVue—collaborative development and hybrid visual programming with the use of a visual formalism-based extension language. To create an "org chart" using ACE, an end user would begin with a graph visual formalism. She would then create nodes for individuals in the organization and link them together with the built-in editing operations provided by the graph (see figure 7.5). To keep track of the number of people in the organization, the user would create a "head-count" variable as an integer object and attach a formula to a node in the graph using the extension language. A simple string object "Head-count" labels the integer node that contains the headcount and formula. The formula attached to Node [5] is:

[5 − − > SetValue] = number-of(ExpandNode ([0])

where Node [0] is the root node representing Sue.

Note that in the org chart the extension language refers to nodes in a graph, analogous to the cells in a table that a spreadsheet formula language references. It is a natural way for an end user to think of making a calculation over information that is best represented in a graph, that is, perform a calculation over the nodes in this branch of the tree starting with a given node. The graph provides a clear visualization of application state, and the user need only click on the appropriate nodes to enter the formula.

To develop this application, the end user might start by creating the nodes for individuals as string objects. But then she might discover that she wants a more complex representation, something like a "person object." To create this new datatype, she can start with a panel visual formalism, as shown in figure 7.6.

She creates the appropriate fields as integer and string objects, giving a concrete example of a person in the application (here John Q. Jones). She then invokes the ACE operation "make into prototype" and supplies a datatype name. Now ACE "knows about" person objects, and they appear in the system as standard semantic types such as string or integer. Their components can be accessed through the extension language. She can add fields to the prototype as she discovers more about what she wants a person object to be.

Our user may now find that she wants a more complex user interface showing only selected aspects of the person object. In fact, she wants something like figure 7.7 in which a panel with an individual's name allows the user to browse to a presentation of the person with birthdate, gender, and address fields shown. This is more than she knows how to build interactively using the ACE panel. To achieve this user interface, the end user asks a programmer to help her. This aspect of the development of the person object is an example of collaborative programming in which the user successively refines her idea of what she wants in the application, working both independently and with a programmer when she has reached the limits of her abilities.

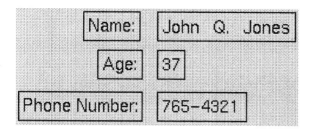

Figure 7.6
A person object

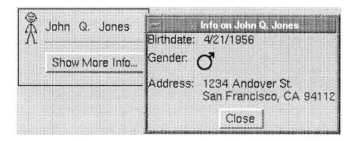

Figure 7.7
A person object created by a C++ programmer

After considering these examples, a more detailed diagram of the ACE architecture will make more sense (see figure 7.8). Note the different modules for different kinds of collaborating users.

* * *

As we hope we have conveyed in this book, the extension of computational power to end users is but "a small matter of programming." This is true for end users themselves, who will, with the right tools, abolish the distinction between "end user" and "programmer." It is also true for researchers, designers, and developers who see the promise and fascination of working on solutions to the problems of end user computing. It is encouraging that efforts to promote end user programming are underway at large companies such as Hewlett-Packard, DEC, Xerox, Schlumberger, and Apple Computer; at small start-ups such as Interval Research of Palo Alto; and at universities such as Carnegie Mellon, University of Michigan, Fordham, Loughborough University of Technology, and Cambridge

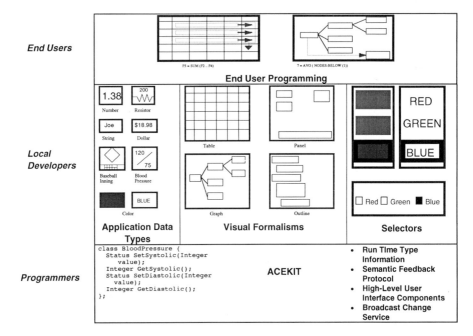

ACE Architecture

Figure 7.8
ACE architecture

University. The collective perspectives and talents in these diverse organizations will surely lead to advances in end user computing in the near future.

We have learned from our studies of end user computing by casting a wide net, looking across a variety of everyday activities, taking into account what people accomplish with such quotidian artifacts as slit-gongs, baseball scoresheets, and knitting patterns, as well as by paying careful attention to the use of successful end user programming systems. Our interactions with users of a variety of end user programming systems, including spreadsheets, CAD systems, and Logo, give us reason to believe that, in time, we can and will fulfill the true potential of computing machines, to make our everyday lives and work more efficient, effective, creative, and pleasurable.

Appendix

Spreadsheet Study Questions

1. What do you do here (i.e. what are the tasks of your job)?
2. What do you do with spreadsheets? (This question involved looking at actual spreadsheets on-line and/or in paper copy. We looked at spreadsheet structure, the use of annotations and labels, formula complexity, how spreadsheets are used during meetings, etc. as part of this question.)
3. Who else uses this spreadsheet (of those we talk about in question 2)?
4. How did you create this spreadsheet (of those we talk about in question 2)? Or alternatively, who created it and who else uses it?
5. How accurate is your spreadsheet? How do you know?
6. How do you find errors?
7. How do you fix errors?
8. Are there any problems you tried to solve with spreadsheets where the spreadsheet approach didn't work? If so, what are they, and what were the problems?
9. What is your educational background?
10. What do you like about spreadsheets?
11. What do you dislike about spreadsheets?
12. What would make spreadsheets easier to use?
13. What would else would you like spreadsheets to do?

CAD Study Questions

1. What is your job/position?
2. What is your educational and job-related background?
3. What is the work process/flow, and where does CAD fit in?
4. Do you share your work with others in your group? If so, how? (Do you share CAD files, paper drawings, etc.?)
5. What CAD system(s) do you use? For what function?
6. Has your system been customized? If so, who does it, and what specific customizations have been done?
7. How did you learn to customize (if applicable)?

8. Is there a CAD expert in your group? If so, how did that person get to be the expert?

9. What do you like/dislike about the system you use?

10. What would make it easier to use your system (manuals, better organized program, etc.)? What other features would you like to see?

Notes

Chapter 1

1. To solve the knotty problem of gender-specific language, I sometimes use "he" as the generic and sometimes "she." Sentences that hew to a strict "he or she" construction get bogged down when any complexity sets in, and the reader is forced to negotiate a thicket of "he or she" 's, and "his or her" 's.

2. Thanks to Thomas Green for supplying the graffito.

3. After doing the spreadsheet study, we recognized that collaboration was important and that we should ask about it in the CAD study. However, in the CAD study we found an entirely new pattern of collaboration that we then had to explore. These findings are discussed in chapter 6.

4. In ethnographic studies, participants are called "informants" in the sense that they are to *inform* the investigator, rather than that the investigator is to *subject* participants to an experiment (as in psychology), in which case they are subjects. The essential notion is that the anthropologist is ignorant of the understandings possessed by the informant but wishes to learn as much as possible through interaction and observation.

5. Lotus and 1-2-3 are registered trademarks of Lotus Development Corporation. Microsoft and Excel are registered trademarks of Microsoft Corporation. HP ME30 is a product of Hewlett-Packard.

6. HyperCard is a registered trademark of Apple Computer, Metaphor Capsule is a registered trademark of Metaphor Systems, Inc. Mathematica is a registered trademark of Wolfram Research, Inc.

Chapter 2

1. Conversation analysts refer to informal everyday conversations as "mundane" conversations, and I will adopt that convention here. The contrast is to more formal verbal communication such as a lecture or speech.

2. Shelley recounts Frankenstein's ruminations as he prepares to create a human being after an initial success in acquiring "the capacity to bestow animation":

> I doubted at first whether I should attempt the creation of a being like myself, or one of simpler organization; but my imagination was too much exalted by my first success to permit me to doubt of my ability to give life to an animal as

complex and wonderful as man. The materials at present within my command hardly appeared adequate to so arduous an undertaking, but I doubted not that I should ultimately succeed. I prepared myself for a multitude of reverses . . . yet when I considered the improvement which every day takes place in science and mechanics, I was encouraged to hope my present attempts would at least lay the foundations of future success. Nor could I consider the magnitude and complexity of my plan as any argument of its impracticality.

3. Such control of turns is, however, characteristic of other communicative contexts such as chastising children, which has quite the flavor of the courtroom ("Don't speak until you're spoken to!"). Such communication seems to have more in common with the formal communication Atkinson writes about than with mundane conversation. Though conversation analysts claim that children are socialized through mundane conversation (see Goodwin and Heritage, 1990), this assumption would seem to call for empirical evaluation.

4. This particular interpretation of Holstein's (1988) data differs from his own.

5. Holstein (1988) provided fictitious patient names, which I have used here. His transcription conventions are slightly modified here to highlight our points and avoid distracting technical detail.

6. The functional importance of the kind of structured legal communication described by Atkinson (1990) can be well appreciated by considering what a trial would be like in its absence. In 1991, the American public was subjected to just such a spectacle during the confirmation hearings for Clarence Thomas's nomination to the Supreme Court. Thomas was accused by a former employee, Anita Hill, of sexual harassment, charges brought forward in the hearings. During the hearings, the lack of established communicative procedures, which included lack of rules for examining and cross-examining witnesses and lack of evidentiary procedure and standards, meant that the hearings, which became a mock trial of the worst sort, proceeded on innuendo, political posturing, and highly unusual forms of legal communication, including dramatic readings from authoritative tomes such as *The Exorcist* and psychoanalyses of Anita Hill and Clarence Thomas freely proferred by completely untrained individuals.

Chapter 3

1. Pig Latin ("Ig-pay, Atin-lay") is chiefly useful for a brief time against younger children before they (quickly) catch on to the rules by which Pig Latin sentences are produced.

2. See Lave (1988) on the personalistic use of formal systems. She observes that people create their own personal ways of treating culturally agreed upon formal systems such as money. For example, she discusses the notion of "mad money" reported by some of the informants in the studies she cites, in which individuals make up their own rules about handling some portion of their money. People do create their own versions of formal systems for some purposes, but these same people also operate in the standard mode of the system as well; for example, even someone who keeps a stash of "mad money" balances her checkbook using standard arithmetic procedures and repays loans according to agreed upon means of computing the balance of the loan.

3. Anthropologists, of course, have created notations to formally model the kinship systems they study.

4. We are using the Little League version of the scoresheet notation here.

5. Figure 3.3 shows only 14; however, in actual use another symbol, "KS," is used, which stands for strike out swinging.

6. Typographical conventions from the printed pattern have been preserved in showing the pattern here.

7. Games are not confined to modern Western culture; all cultures have games, and even in preliterate cultures the rules of games may be very complex (see Cole and Scribner, 1974). Of course there are also "games" such as the medieval Florentine *Calcio Storico*, a kind of no-holds-barred soccer, in which the only rule is that players are not allowed to kick an unconscious adversary. The game is still played annually in Florence. Even in this highly unconstrained setting we find the structure of teams, the notion of a goal and a playing field, a time limit, referees, uniforms, a trophy. What is essentially a riot proceeds according to centuries-old conventions (Jordan, 1991).

8. People may also like many other things about games such as their pageantry, getting to know specific players, and so forth. However, the understanding of the game and its possibilities are paramount for the serious audience.

9. An RBI is the number of runs batted in, a statistic computed for a batter, and the ERA, or earned run average, is the number of runs a pitcher has allowed without fielding errors. Actually, these statistics are more complicated than this and follow strict rules about what counts and does not count as an RBI or ERA, as well as being computed over a defined time span. (See Waggoner, Moloney and Howard, 1987 for details.)

10. We refer specifically to the spreadsheet formula language. Spreadsheets also have macro languages, but they are used by many fewer users and do not constitute the basic interface to spreadsheet functionality that we are concerned with at this point in the discussion.

11. FrameMaker is a registered trademark of Frame Technologies, Inc.

12. PowerPoint is a trademark of Microsoft.

13. HyperTalk is a registered trademark of Apple Computer.

14. No disrespect to GNU Emacs Lisp is intended; it is deservedly popular among trained programmers and embodies many wonderful ideas and much useful functionality.

15. There is stackware available, but it tends to be weighted toward simple index-card-file applications, rather than serious business use. For example, in the Summer 1991 issue of the *Heizer Software* catalogue, which specializes in spreadsheet, HyperCard, and ToolBook applications, typical spreadsheet applications included Beam Analysis 2.0, Complete Construction Cost Estimator, Beef Cowherd Costs and Returns, Asset Management and Financial Independence, Costed Bill of Materials, and Multi-Unit Property Management. By contrast, typical HyperCard applications included Sanskrit Tutor, MacChef, Tarot Pack, HomeBrew and Brew Records, Baby Names, and Golf Doctor.

Chapter 4

1. LabView is a registered trademark of National Instruments, Inc. VEE is a registered trademark of Hewlett-Packard. It stands for "Visual Engineering Environment." Prograph is a registered trademark of TGSSystems

2. SeeMore is a registered trademark of Personics, Inc. WideView is a registered trademark of Spies Laboratories.

3. Example modification is not the same as the use of didactic examples, which have an important role in learning and enhancing skill in programming (and many other areas of endeavor). Didactic examples are especially helpful in learning language syntax as part of a larger program of study in which the fundamental concepts of a programming language are learned.

4. Myers (1990b) suggested a taxonomy of different kinds of programming by example systems, including those that do and do not use inferencing. We are discussing the state-of-the-art inferencing systems here.

5. Adobe Illustrator and Claris MacDraw can do this.

6. WorldBuilder is a registered trademark of Silicon Beach Software Inc.

Chapter 5

1. Of course there may come a day when many of us are provisioned with much larger screens in our workspaces. But a countervailing force is toward small-sized computers that we can easily carry with us, the size of the human body providing an absolute constraint. Workspaces also appear to be moving toward smaller, not larger, square footage, as employers attempt to hold down costs in today's extremely competitive market (*San Jose Mercury News*, October 15, 1990, p. B1).

2. In our study the largest spreadsheets had about a thousand rows.

3. This particular notational convention happens to be that of Lotus 1-2-3. Other spreadsheets may use a slightly different notation, but all can express cell relations as aspects of tabular structure.

4. Green (1989) believes that problems showing, tracking, and changing dependencies are common to many programming problems. He calls the difficulty "viscosity" in the sense that making changes where there are dependencies is slow and sticky because it is often hard to find the source of a dependency, or to know the possible effects of a change.

5. Many researchers have been disappointed that Logo has not been more successful in teaching children difficult programming concepts such as recursion, and in teaching "higher-level" thinking skills (much as the learning of Latin was once said to do) (Pea and Sheingold, 1987). However these disappointments seem to stem from unrealistic expectations, rather than from the fact that Logo is not useful. Children in the nine- to eleven-year-old range (typical Logo users) are still learning basic logical forms in everyday language use and cannot be expected to quickly grasp conditionals, much less recursion. Pea and Kurland (1987) also point out that, "Educators often assume that adult programmers are not beleaguered by conceptual problems in their programming, but . . . they are. Once we recognize that programming by 'intellectually mature' adults is not characterized by error-free, routine performances, we might better understand difficulties of children learning to program, who devote only small amounts of their school time to learning to program." And of course, as with any subject, there is wide variation in the interests and abilities students bring to the study of Logo.

Some also believe that more structured teaching methods may be needed to effectively teach programming to children (Pea and Sheingold, 1987). Early experiences were skewed to an "exploratory" approach in which at least some children did not receive adequate guidance. In informal observations that I have conducted at Bubb Elementary School in Mountain View, California, I have seen evidence (albeit limited to one fifth grade public school computer science class) that a more structured approach can be effective. The children are told that "everyone can learn to program" and they are given careful instruction in Logo language concepts (rather than being left to "explore" without guidance). Emphasis is on basic concepts of variables, procedures, and iteration. Conditionals are covered near the end of the year for those children who are ready.

Chapter 6

1. See Mackay (1990b) on Project Athena.

2. Ralph Kimball works for Application Design Incorporated of Los Gatos, California and consults on many kinds of software applications. Metaphor Capsule is an end user programming system from Metaphor, Inc. of Mountain View, California. It lets users link spreadsheets, databases, documents, and so forth, by connecting icons together. Effectively, users are "piping" data from one form to another, for example, a database query to a spreadsheet to a graph. Metaphor Capsule supports programming features such as encapsulation and iteration.

3. AutoLISP is a subset of XLISP and Common LISP, with some additional functions to support design tasks.

4. No criticism of the programmers in Mackay's study is intended in any way; they had no charter to create end user customizations.

Chapter 7

1. CareVue is a registered trademark of Hewlett-Packard.

References

Allen, C. (1992). Reciprocal evolution: A design and research strategy for the development and integration of basic research design and studies of work practices. In D. Schuler and A. Namioka, eds., *Participatory Design: Principles and Practices*. Hillsdale, NJ: Lawrence Erlbaum Associates.

Andreae, P. (1985). Justified generalization: Acquiring procedures from examples. Ph.D. dissertation, Department of Electrical Engineering and Computer Science, MIT.

Arganbright, D. (1986). Mathematical modeling with spreadsheets. *Abacus 3*, 18–31.

Atkinson, J. (1982). Understanding formality. *British Journal of Sociology 33*, 86–117.

Atkinson, J. (1990). A comparative analysis of formal and informal courtroom interaction. In P. Drew and J. Heritage, eds., *Talk at Work*. Cambridge: Cambridge University Press.

Bar-On, E., Or-Bach, R. and Ranney, M. (1991). A learning environment that promotes distributed problem solving. Paper presented at SESAME/EMST Colloquium, University of California, Berkeley. Available from first author at Department of Science Education, Technion University, Haifa, Israel.

Bear, S., Coleman, D. and Hayes, F. (1989). Introducing objectcharts, or how to use statecharts in object-oriented design, HPL-Report-ISC-TM-89-167. Bristol, England: Hewlett-Packard Laboratories.

Berlin, L. (1990). When objects collide: Experience with reusing multiple class hierarchies. In *OOPSLA/ECOOP '90 Proceedings*. Ottawa, Canada, 21–25 October. Pp. 181–193.

Berlin, L. and O'Day, V. (1990). Platform and application issues in multi-user hypertext. In S. Gibbs, ed., *Proceedings of the IFIP WG 8.4 Conference on Multi-User Interfaces and Applications*. Heraklion, Crete, Greece, 24–26 September. Amsterdam: Elsevier Science Publishers.

Bernard, P. and Marcel, T. (1984). Representation and understanding in the use of symbols and pictograms. In R. Easterley and H. Zwaga, eds., *Information Design*. New York: Wiley and Sons.

Blomberg, J., Giacomi, J., Mosher, A. and Swenton-Wall, P. (1992). Ethnographic field methods and their relation to design. In D. Schuler and A. Namioka, eds., *Participatory Design: Principles and Practices*. Hillsdale, NJ: Lawrence Erlbaum Associates.

Blumofe, R. and Hecht, A. (1988). Executing real-time structured analysis specifications. *ACM SIGSOFT Software Engineering Notes*, 13, 32–40.

Bødker, S. (1989). A human activity approach to user interfaces. *Human-computer Interaction* 4, 171–195.

Bolt, R. (1984). *The Human Interface*. Belmont, CA: Wadsworth.

Bowen, W. (1989). The puny payoff from office computers. In T. Forester, ed. *Computers in the Human Context*. New York: Basil Blackwell. Pp. 267–271.

Brooks, F. (1987). No silver bullet: Essence and accidents of software engineering. *IEEE Computer* 20, 10–19.

Brooks, L. and Wells, C. (1989). Role conflict in design supervision. *IEEE Transactions on Engineering Management* 36, 271–281.

Brooks, R. (1991). Comparative task analysis: An alternative direction for human-computer interaction science. In J. Carroll, ed., *Designing Interaction: Psychology at the Human-Computer Interface*. Cambridge: Cambridge University Press.

Brown, P. and Gould, J. (1987). How people create spreadsheets. *ACM Transactions on Office Information Systems* 5, 258–272.

Button, G. (1990). Going up a blind alley. In P. Luff, N. Gilbert and D. Frolich, eds., *Computers and Conversation*. London: Academic Press. Pp. 67–90.

Buxton, W. (1987). The "natural" language of interaction: A perspective on nonverbal dialogue. In *Proceedings of CIPS*, pp. 311–316.

Card, S., Moran, T. and Newell, A. (1983). *The Psychology of Human-Computer Interaction*. Hillsdale, NJ: Lawrence Erlbaum Associates.

Carroll, L. (1936). *The Complete Works of Lewis Carroll*. New York: Modern Library.

Casner, S. (1991). A task-analytic approach to the automated design of graphic presentations. *ACM Transactions on Graphics* 10, 111–151.

Chang, S. (1990). *Visual Languages and Visual Programming*. New York: Plenum Press.

Chang, S., Ichikawa, T. and Ligomenides, P. (1986). *Visual Languages*. New York: Plenum Press.

Chapanis, A. (1975). Interactive human communication. *Scientific American* 232, 34–42.

Ciccarelli, E. and Nardi, B. (1988). Browsing schematics: Query-filtered graphs with context nodes. In *Proceedings of the Second Annual Workshop on Space Operations, Automation and Robotics (SOAR '88)*. Dayton, OH, 20–23 July. Pp. 193–204.

Clement, A. (1990). Cooperative support for computer work: A social perspective on the empowering of end users. In *Proceedings of the Conference on Computer-Supported Cooperative Work*. Los Angeles, CA, 7–10 October. Pp. 223–236.

Cleveland, W. (1985). *The Elements of Graphing Data*. Monterey, CA: Wadsworth Advanced Books.

Cleveland, W. (1990). A model for graphical perception. AT&T Statistics Research Report. Murray Hill, NJ: AT&T Bell Labs.

Cole, M. and Scribner, S. (1974). *Culture and Thought*. New York: Wiley.

Cozy Afghans (1989). Volume 843. Pickens, SC: Brunswick Worsted Mills Inc.

Creech, M., Freeze, D. and Griss, M. (1991). Using hypertext in selecting reusable software components. HPLabs Tech Report HPL-91-59. Palo Alto: Hewlett-Packard Laboratories.

Cunniff, N., Taylor, R. and Black, J. (1986). Does programming language affect the type of conceptual bugs in beginners' programs? A comparison of FPL and Pascal. In M. Mantei and P. Orberton, eds., *Proceedings CHI '86 Conference*.

Cunniff, N. and Taylor, R. (1987). Graphics and learning: A study of learner characteristics and comprehension of programming languages. In H.-J. Bullinger and B. Shackel, eds., *Proceedings INTERACT '87*.

Curtis, B. (1989). Five paradigms in the psychology of programming. In M. Helander, ed., *Handbook of Human-Computer Interaction*. Amsterdam: Elsevier Science Publishers.

Cypher, A. (1991). Eager: Programming repetitive tasks by example. In *Proceedings CHI '91*. New Orleans, LA, 27 April–2 May. Pp. 33–39.

D'Andrade, R. (1981). The cultural part of cognition. *Cognitive Science 5*, 179–195.

D'Andrade, R. (1989). Culturally based reasoning. In A. Gellatly, D. Rogers and J. Sloboda, eds., *Cognition and Social Worlds*. Oxford: Clarendon Press.

Davies, S. (1991). Characterizing program design activity: Neither strictly top-down nor globally opportunistic. *Behavior and Information Technology 10*, 173–190.

Davydov, V., Zinchenko, V. and Talyzina, N. (1982). The problem of activity in the works of A. N. Leont'ev. *Soviet Psychology 21*, 31–42.

de Baar, D., Foley, J. and Mullet, K. (1992). Coupling application design and user interface design. In *Proceedings CHI '92*. Monterey, CA, 3–7 May. Pp. 259–272.

Detienne, F. (1990). Difficulties in designing with an object-oriented programming language. In *Proceedings INTERACT '90*. Cambridge, England, 27–31 August.

Domingue, J. (1990). Compressing and comparing metric execution spaces. *Proceedings INTERACT '90*. Cambridge, England, 27–31 August.

Doyle, J. (1990). Naive users and the Lotus interface: A field study. *Behavior and Information Technology 9*, 81–89.

Du Boulay, B. (1989). Some difficulties of learning to program. In E. Soloway and J. Spohrer, eds., *Studying the Novice Programmer*. Hillsdale, NJ: Lawrence Erlbaum Associates. Pp. 282–300.

Dunlop, C. and Kling, R. (1991). Introduction: Social controversies about computerization. In C. Dunlop and R. Kling, eds., *Computerization and Controversy*. Boston: Academic Press.

Eason, K. (1988). *Information Technology and Organizational Change*. New York: Taylor and Francis, Ltd.

Eisenstadt, M., Domingue, J., Rajan, T. and Motta, E. (1990). Visual knowledge engineering. *IEEE Transactions on Software Engineering* 16, 1164–1177.

Engeström, Y. and Middleton, D. (1992). *Cognition and Communication at Work*. Cambridge: Cambridge University Press.

Fikes, R. and Nilsson, N. (1971). STRIPS: A new approach to the application of theorem proving to problem solving. *Artificial Intelligence* 2, 189–205.

Fitter, M. and Green, T. R. G. (1979). When do diagrams make good computer languages? *International Journal of Man-Machine Studies* 11, 235–261.

Fletcher, K. (1987). Evaluation and choice as a satisficing process. *Journal of Marketing Management*, 3, 13–23.

Flor, N. and Hutchins, E. (1991). Analyzing distributed cognition in software teams: A case study of team programming during perfective software maintenance. In J. Koenemann-Belliveau et al., eds., *Proceedings of the Fourth Annual Workshop on Empirical Studies of Programmers*. Norwood, NJ: Ablex Publishing. Pp. 36–59.

Floyd, C., Züllighoven, H., Budde R. and Keil-Slawik, R., eds., (1992). *Software Development and Reality Construction*. Berlin: Springer-Verlag.

Forester, T. (1989). *Computers in the Human Context*. New York: Basil Blackwell.

Franke, R. (1989). Technological revolution and productivity decline: The case of US banks. In T. Forester, ed., *Computers in the Human Context*. New York: Basil Blackwell. Pp. 281–290.

Frolich, D. and Luff, P. (1990). Applying the technology of conversation to the technology for conversation. In P. Luff, N. Gilbert and D. Frolich, eds., *Computers and Conversation*. London: Academic Press. Pp. 187–220.

Furnas, G. (1986). Generalized fisheye views. In *Proceedings of CHI '86, Conference on Human Factors in Computing Systems*. Boston, 13–17 April. Pp. 13–17.

Gantt, M. and Nardi, B. (1992). Gardeners and gurus: Patterns of cooperation among CAD users. In *Proceedings CHI '92*. Monterey, CA, 3–7 May. Pp. 107–117.

Gardner, H. (1985). *The Mind's New Science*. New York: Basic Books.

Garfinkel, H. (1967). *Studies in Ethnomethodology*. Englewood Cliffs, NJ: Prentice-Hall.

Glaser, B. and Strauss, A. (1967). *The Discovery of Grounded Theory: Strategies for Qualitative Research*. New York: Aldine Publishing Co.

Glinert, E. (1989). An In-Depth Look at Selected Visual Systems. In *Proceedings of CHI '89*. Austin, Texas. Workshop on Visual Computing Environments. Pp. 194–200.

Goodwin, C. and Heritage, J. (1990). Conversation analysis. *Annual Review of Anthropology* 19, 283–307.

Gould, J. (1988). How to design usable systems. In M. Helander, ed., *Handbook of Human-Computer Interaction*. Amsterdam: Elsevier Science Publishers. Pp. 757–789.

Gould, J, Boies, S. and Lewis, C. (1991). Making usable, useful, productivity-enhancing computer applications. *Communications of the ACM* 34, 75–85.

Green, T. R. G. (1982). Pictures of programs and other processes, or how to do things with lines. *Behaviour and Information Technology* 1, 3–36.

Green, T. R. G. (1989). Cognitive dimensions of notations. In A. Sutcliffe and L. Macaulay, eds., *People and Computers V*. Cambridge: Cambridge University Press.

Green, T. R .G. (1990a). The nature of programming. In J-M. Hoc, T. R. G. Green, R. Samurcay and D. Gilmore, eds., *Psychology of Programming*. London: Academic Press.

Green, T. R. G. (1990b). Programming languages as information structures. In J-M. Hoc, T. R. G. Green, R. Samurcay and D. Gilmore, eds., *Psychology of Programming*. London: Academic Press.

Green, T. R. G., Petre, M. and Bellamy, R. (1991). Comprehensibility of visual and textual programs: A test of superlativism against the "match-mismatch" conjecture. In J. Koenemann-Belliveau, T. Moher and S. Robertson, eds., *Empirical Studies of Programmers: Fourth Workshop*. Norwood, NJ: Ablex. Pp. 121–146.

Greenberg, S. and Witten, I. (1988). How users repeat their actions on computers: Principles for design of history mechanisms. In *Proceedings CHI '88*. Washington, D.C., May.

Greenblatt, D. and Waxman, J. (1978). A study of three database query languages. In B. Shneiderman, ed., *Databases: Improving Usability and Responsiveness*. New York: Academic Press.

Greif, I. (1982). The user interface of a personal calendar program. In *Proceedings NYU Symposium on User Interfaces*. Pp. 207–222.

Grice, H. (1975). *Logic and Conversation*. New York: Dickenson Publishing.

Grudin, J. (1989). The case against user interface consistency. *Communications of the ACM* 32, 1164–1173.

Guindon, R. (1988). Software design tasks as ill-structured problems, software design as an opportunistic process. MCC Technical Report No. STP-214-88. Austin, TX: MCC.

Haeberli, P. (1988). ConMan: A visual programming language for interactive graphics. *ACM Computer Graphics* 22, 103–111.

Harel, D. (1988). On visual formalisms, *Communications of the ACM* 31, 514–520.

Harwood, K. (1987). On prototyping and the role of the software engineer. *ACM SIGSOFT, Software Engineering Notes* 12, 34.

Hayes, P. and Reddy, D. (1983). Steps toward graceful interaction in spoken and written man-machine communication. *International Journal of Man-Machine Studies* 19, 231–284.

Hayes, P. and Szekeley, P. (1983). Graceful interaction through the COUSIN command interface. *International Journal of Man-Machine Studies* 19, 285–306.

Heritage, J. (1984). *Garfinkel and Ethnomethodology.* Cambridge: Polity Press.

Heydon, A., Maimone, M., Tygar, J., Wing, J. and Zaremski, A. (1989). Constraining pictures with pictures. In *Proceedings of IFIPS'89.* San Francisco, CA, August. Pp. 157–162.

Hoc, J. (1989). Do we really have conditional statements in our brains? In E. Soloway and J. Spohrer, eds., *Studying the Novice Programmer.* Hillsdale, NJ: Lawrence Erlbaum Associates. Pp. 179–190.

Holstein, J. (1988). Court ordered incompetence: Conversational organization in involuntary commitment hearings. *Social Problems* 35, 458–473.

Hutchins, E. (1987). Metaphors for interface design. ICS Report 8703. La Jolla: University of California, San Diego.

Hutchins, E. (1990a). Getting it straight in Trobriand Island land litigation. In K. Watson-Gegeo and G. White, eds., *Disentangling Conflict Discourse in Pacific Societies.* Stanford CA: Stanford University Press. Pp. 412–458.

Hutchins, E. (1990b). The technology of team navigation. In J. Galegher, ed., *Intellectual Teamwork.* Hillsdale, NJ: Lawrence Erlbaum.

Hutchins, E. (1991a). How a cockpit remembers its speeds. Manuscript. La Jolla, CA: University of California, Department of Cognitive Science.

Hutchins, E. (1991b). The social organization of distributed cognition. In L. Resnick, ed., *Perspectives on Socially Shared Cognition.* Washington, DC: American Psychological Association. Pp. 283–307.

Hutchins, E., Hollan, J. and Norman, D. (1986). Direct manipulation interfaces. In D. Norman and S. Draper, eds., *User Centered System Design.* Hillsdale, NJ: Erlbaum Publishers.

ITC (1988). *The Andrew System.* Information Technology Center. Pittsburgh, PA: Carnegie Mellon University.

Jeffries, R. and Rosenberg, J. (1987). Comparing a form-based and a language-based user interface for instructing a mail program. In *Proceedings CHI+GI '87.* Toronto, 5–9 April. Pp. 261–266.

Johnson, B. and Shneiderman, B. (1991). Tree-maps: A space-filling approach to the visualization of hierarchical information structures. In *Proceedings Visualization '91*. San Diego. Pp. 284–291.

Johnson, J. (1992). Selectors: Going beyond user-interface widgets. In *Proceedings CHI '92*, Monterey, CA, 3–7 May. Pp. 273–279.

Johnson, J., Nardi, B., Zarmer, C. and Miller, J. (1993). ACE: A new approach to building interactive graphical applications. *Communications of the ACM 36* (April).

Johnson-Laird, P. (1983). *Mental models*. Cambridge: Cambridge University Press.

Johnson-Laird, P. and Wason, P. (1970). A theoretical analysis of insight into a reasoning task. *Cognitive Psychology* 1, 134–148.

Jordan, P. (1991). Made to be broken. American Way Magazine, November. Pp. 72–78, 126–128.

Kahney, H. (1989). What do novice programmers know about recursion? In E. Soloway and J. Spohrer, eds., *Studying the Novice Programmer*. Hillsdale, NJ: Lawrence Erlbaum Associates. Pp. 209–228.

Kay, A. (1984). Computer software. *Scientific American 5*, 53–59.

Kay, A. (1991). Computers, networks and education. *Scientific American* September. Pp. 138–148.

Kessler, C. and Anderson, J. (1989). Learning flow of control: Recursive and iterative procedures. In E. Soloway and J. Spohrer, eds., *Studying the Novice Programmer*. Hillsdale, NJ: Lawrence Erlbaum Associates. Pp. 229–260.

Kuutti, K. (1991). Activity theory and its applications to information systems research and development. In H.-E. Nissen, ed., *Information Systems Research*. Amsterdam: Elsevier Science Publishers. Pp. 529–549.

Ladret, D. and Rueher, M. (1991). VLP: A visual logic programming language. *Journal of Visual Languages and Computing* 2, 163–188.

Larkin, J. and Simon, H. (1987). Why a diagram is (sometimes) worth ten thousand words, *Cognitive Science* 11, 65–100.

Lau-Kee, D. (1990). Visual and by-example interactive systems for non-programmers. YCST 90/03. York, England: University of York, Department of Computer Science.

Lave, J. (1988). *Cognition in Practice*. Cambridge: Cambridge University Press.

Lee, D. (1986). Usage patterns and sources of assistance for personal computer users. *MIS Quarterly*, December. Pp. 313–325.

Leont'ev, A. (1974). The problem of activity in psychology. *Soviet Psychology* 13, 2, 4–33.

Leont'ev, A. (1978). *Activity, consciousness, and personality*. Englewood Cliffs, NJ: Prentice Hall.

Levinson, S. (1983). *Pragmatics*. Cambridge: Cambridge University Press.

Levy, S. (1984). A spreadsheet way of knowledge. *Harper's*. November. Pp. 58–64.

Lewis, G. and Olson, G. (1987). Can principles of cognition lower the barriers to programming? In *Empirical Studies of Programmers: Second Workshop*. Norwood, NJ: Ablex. Pp. 248–263.

Luff, P., Gilbert, N. and Frolich, D., eds., (1990). *Computers and Conversation*. London: Academic Press.

Mackay, W. (1990a). Patterns of sharing customizable software. In *Proceedings of the Conference on Computer-Supported Cooperative Work*. Los Angeles, 7–10 October. Pp. 209–221.

Mackay, W. (1990b). Users and customizable software. A co-adaptive phenomenon. Ph.D. dissertation. Sloan School of Management. MIT, Cambridge, MA.

MacLean, A., Carter, K., Lovstrand, L. and Moran, T. (1990). User-tailorable systems: Pressing the issues with buttons. In *Proceedings, CHI '90*. Seattle, 1–5 April. Pp. 175–182.

Marques, D., Dallemagne, G., Klinker, G., McDermott, J. and Tung, D. (1992). Easy programming: Empowering people to build their own applications. *IEEE Expert*. June. Pp. 16–29.

Martin, J. (1967). *Design of Real-time Computer Systems*. Englewood Cliffs, NJ: Prentice-Hall.

Maulsby, D. (1988). Inducing procedures interactively. Master's thesis. Department of Computer Science, University of Calgary, Calgary.

Maulsby, D., Witten, I. and Kittlitz, K. (1989). Metamouse: Specifying graphical procedures by example. *Computer Graphics* 23, 127–136.

Myers, B. (1989a). Introduction to visual programming and program visualization. In *Proceedings of CHI '89*. Austin, Texas. Workshop on Visual Computing Environments.

Myers, B. (1989b). Evaluation of visual programming and program visualization. *Proceedings of CHI '89*. Austin, Texas. Workshop on Visual Computing Environments.

Myers, B. (1990a). Demonstrational Interfaces: A Step Beyond Direct Manipulation. Technical report CMU-CS-90-162. Pittsburgh, PA: Carnegie Mellon University.

Myers, B. (1990b). Taxonomies of visual programming and program visualization. *Journal of Visual Languages and Computing* 1, 97–123.

Myers, B. (1991). Text formatting by demonstration. In *Proceedings CHI '91*. New Orleans, LA, 27 April–2 May. Pp. 251–256.

Myers, B. (1992). *Languages for Developing User Interfaces*. Boston: Jones and Bartlett.

Myers, B., Giuse, D., Dannenberg, R., VanderZanden, B., Kosbie, D., Pervin, E., Mickish, A. and Marchal, P. (1990). Comprehensive support for graphical, highly-interactive user interfaces: The Garnet User Interface Development Environment. *IEEE Computer* 23, 71–85.

Napier, H., Lane, D., Batsell, R. and Guadango, N. (1989). Impact of a restricted natural language interface on ease of learning and productivity. *Communications of the ACM* 32, 1190–1198.

Nardi, B. (1992). Studying context: A comparison of activity theory, situated action models, and distributed cognition. In *Proceedings, St. Petersburg Human-Computer Interaction Workshop*. St. Petersburg, Russia, 4–8 August. Pp. 352–359.

Nardi, B. and Miller, J. (1990). The spreadsheet interface: A basis for end user programming, *Proceedings Interact '90*. Cambridge, England, 27–31 August. Pp. 977–983.

Nardi, B. and Miller, J. (1991). Twinkling lights and nested loops: Distributed problem solving and spreadsheet development. *International Journal of Man-Machine Studies* 34, 161–184.

Nardi, B. and Zarmer, C. (1993). Beyond models and metaphors: Visual formalisms in user interface design. *Journal of Visual Languages and Computing*, March.

Neal, L. (1989). A system for example-based programming. In *Proceedings of CHI '89, Conference on Human Factors in Computing Systems*. Austin, TX, 30 April–4 May.

Nelson, R. and Cheney, P. (1987). Training end users: An exploratory study. *MIS Quarterly*, December. Pp. 546–559.

Newell, A. and Simon, H. (1972). *Human Problem Solving*. Englewood Cliffs, NJ: Prentice Hall.

Norman, D. (1988). *The Psychology of Everyday Things*. New York: Basic Books.

Norman, D. (1991). Cognitive artifacts. in J. Carroll, ed., *Designing Interaction: Psychology at the Human-Computer Interface*. New York: Cambridge University Press.

Norman, D. and Hutchins, E. (1988). Computation via direct manipulation. Final Report to Office of Naval Research, Contract No. N00014-85-C-0133. La Jolla: University of California, San Diego.

Norman, M. and Thomas, P. (1990). The very idea. In P. Luff, N. Gilbert and D. Frolich, eds., *Computers and Conversation*. London: Academic Press. Pp. 51–65.

Nygren, E., Lind, M. Johnson, M. and Sandblad, B. (1992). The art of the obvious. In *Proceedings CHI '92*. Monterey, CA, 3–7 May. Pp. 235–239.

Olsen, D., McNeill, T. and Michell, D. (1992). Workspaces: An architecture for editing collections of objects. In *Proceedings CHI '92*. Monterey, CA, 3–7 May. Pp. 267–272.

Olson, J. and Nilsen, E. (1987). Analysis of the cognition involved in spreadsheet software interaction. *Human-Computer Interaction* 3, 309–349.

Panko, R. (1988). *End User Computing: Management, Applications, and Technology.* New York: John Wiley and Sons.

Parker, J. (1992). Mosaic: Animated visual programming for end users. HPL-92-103. Bristol, England: Hewlett-Packard Laboratories.

Pea, R. and Kurland, M. (1987). On the cognitive effects of learning computer programming. In R. Pea and K. Sheingold, eds., *Mirrors of Minds: Patterns of Experience in Educational Computing.* Norwood, NJ: Ablex. Pp. 147–177.

Pea, R. and Sheingold, K. (1987). *Mirrors of Minds: Patterns of Experience in Educational Computing.* Norwood, NJ: Ablex.

Petre, M. and Green, T. R. G. (1990). Where to draw the line with text: Some claims by logic designers about graphics in notation. In *Proceedings INTERACT '90.* Cambridge, England, 27–31 August.

Petre, M. and Green, T. R. G. (1991). Requirements of graphical notations for professional users: Electronics CAD systems as a case study. *Le Travail Humain* 55, 47–70.

Postosnak, K. (1984). Choice of interface modes by empirical groupings of computers users. In *Proceedings INTERACT '84.*

Price-Williams, D. (1962). Abstract and concrete modes of classification in a primitive society. *British Journal of Educational Psychology* 32, 50–61.

Raeithel, A. (1991). Semiotic self-regulation and work: An activity theoretical foundation for design. In R. Floyd et al., eds., *Software Development and Reality Construction.* Berlin: Springer Verlag.

Raymond, D. (1991). Characterizing visual languages In *Proceedings IEEE Workshop on Visual Languages.* Kobe, Japan, 9–11 October. Pp. 176–182.

Rich, E. (1985). Natural language understanding: How natural can it be? In J. Roach, C. Weisbin, M. Tysin and H. Hayman, eds., *The Engineering of Knowledge-Based Systems.* Miami Beach, December. Pp. 372–377.

Robinson, H. (1990) Towards a sociology of human-computer interaction. In P. Luff, N. Gilbert and D. Frolich, eds., *Computers and Conversation.* London: Academic Press. Pp. 39–49.

Rousseau, N. (1990). The Psychology of Programming for Non-programmers. Ph.D. dissertation, Human Sciences Department, Loughborough University, Loughborough, England.

Rousseau, N. (1992a). Patterns of errors made by novice users of structured notations. *Interacting with Computers.* In press.

Rousseau, N. (1992b). A study of end-users evaluating a system: The process and practical implications. Submitted to *Behaviour and Information Technology.*

Sacks, H., Schegloff, E. and Jefferson, G. (1974). A simplest systematics for the organization of turn-taking for conversation. *Language* 50, 696–735.

Sajaniemi, J. and Pekkanen, J. (1988). An empirical analysis of spreadsheet calculation. *Software Practice and Experience* 18, 583–596.

Scharer, L. (1983). User training: Less is more. *Datamation*, July. Pp. 175–182.

Schutz, A. (1962). *Collected Papers. Volume I.* The Hague: Martinus Nijhoff.

Schutz, A. (1964). *Collected Papers. Volume II.* The Hague: Martinus Nijhoff.

Shaiken, H. (1989). The automated factory: Vision and reality. In T. Forester, ed., *Computers in the Human Context.* New York: Basil Blackwell. Pp. 291–300.

Shelley, M. (1963). [1816]. *Frankenstein.* New York: Penguin Books.

Shneiderman, B. (1983). Direct manipulation: a step beyond programming languages. *IEEE Computer* 16, 57–69.

Shu, N. (1984). A forms-oriented and visual directed application development system for non-programmers. In *Proceedings IEEE Computer Society Workshop on Visual Languages.* Hiroshima, Japan. Pp. 162–170.

Shu, N. (1988). A visual programming language designed for automatic programming. In *Proceedings of 21st Hawaii International Conference on System Sciences,* vol. 2.

Software Magazine. (1990). Newsfront: Backlog still flat at 29 months. March issue. P. 12.

Soloway, E., Bonar, J. and Erlich, K. (1989). Cognitive strategies and looping constructs: An empirical study. In E. Soloway and J. Spohrer, eds., *Studying the Novice Programmer.* Hillsdale, NJ: Lawrence Erlbaum Associates. Pp. 191–208.

Soloway, E. and Spohrer, J. (1989). *Studying the Novice Programmer.* Hillsdale, NJ: Lawrence Erlbaum Associates.

Spohrer, J., Soloway, E. and Pope, E. (1989). A goal/plan analysis of buggy Pascal programs. In E. Soloway and J. Spohrer, eds., *Studying the Novice Programmer.* Hillsdale, NJ: Lawrence Erlbaum Associates. Pp. 355–400.

Stallman, R. (1987). *GNU Emacs Lisp Reference.* Cambridge, MA: Free Software Foundation.

Stein, D. (1985). *Ada: A Life and a Legacy.* Cambridge, MA: MIT Press.

Strassman, P. (1990). *The Business Value of Computers.* New Canaan, CT: Information Economics Press.

Suchman, L. (1987). *Plans and Situated Actions.* Cambridge: Cambridge University Press.

Szekeley, P., Luo, P. and Neches, R. (1992). Facilitating the exploration of interface design alternatives: The HUMANOID model of interface design. In *Proceedings CHI '92,* Monterey, CA, 3–7 May. Pp. 507–515.

Tee, C. (1992). Human Factors in Geometric Feature Visualization. Master's thesis, Department of Computer Science and Engineering, MIT, Cambridge, MA.

Tesler, L. (1991). Networked computing in the 1990's. *Scientific American,* September. Pp. 86–93.

Thomas, J. and Gould, J. (1975). A psychological study of query by example. In *Proceedings National Computer Conference*. Arlington, VA.

Thomas, R. (1988). *Advanced Techniques in AutoCAD*. San Francisco: Sybex.

Thomsen, C. (1990). The business instrument panel: A new paradigm for interacting with financial data. In *Proceedings CHI '90*. Seattle, 1–5 April. Pp. 161–166.

Tracy, K. (1991). *Understanding Face-To-Face Interaction*. Hillsdale, NJ: Lawrence Erlbaum Associates.

Trask, M. (1992). End user programming: Oxymoron or holy grail? *Windows Magazine*, April. Pp. 155–156.

Visser, W. (1990). More or less following a plan during design: Opportunistic deviations in specification. *International Journal of Man-Machine Studies 33*, 247–278.

Vlissides, J. and Linton, M. (1990). Unidraw: A framework for building domain-specific graphical editors. *ACM Transactions on Information Systems 8*, 237–268.

Waggoner, G., Moloney, K. and Howard, H. (1987). *Baseball by the Rules*. New York: Taylor Publishing.

Wallace, A. F. C. (1961). *Culture and Personality*. New York: Random House.

Warner, J. (1990). Visual data analysis into the '90s. *Pixel 1*, 40–44.

Warner, T. (1989). Information technology as a competitive burden. In T. Forester, ed., *Computers in the Human Context*. New York: Basil Blackwell. Pp. 273–280.

Wason, P. (1966). Reasoning. In B. Foss, ed., *New Horizons in Psychology*. Middlesex: Penguin.

Wason, P. and Johnson-Laird, P. (1972). *The Psychology of Reasoning*. Cambridge, MA: Harvard University Press.

Wertsch, J., ed. (1981). *The Concept of Activity in Soviet Psychology*. Armonk, NY: Sharpe.

Whitehead, A. (1958). *An Introduction to Mathematics*. New York: Oxford University Press.

Winograd, T. and Flores, F. (1986). *Understanding Computers and Cognition: A New Foundation for Design*. Norwood, NJ: Ablex.

Wolz, U. (1990). The impact of user modeling on text generation in task-centered settings. In *Proceedings Second International Conference on User Modeling*. Honolulu, HI, 29 March–1 April.

Wooffitt, R. (1990). On the analysis of interaction. In P. Luff, N. Gilbert and D. Frolich, eds., *Computers and Conversation*. London: Academic Press. Pp. 7–37.

Wright, P. and Monk, A. (1989). Evaluation for design. In A. Sutcliffe and L. Macaulay, eds., *Proceedings of HCI '89, Fifth BCS HCI Specialist Group conference*. University of Nottingham, September. Cambridge: Cambridge University Press. Pp. 345–358.

Wynn, E. (1980). What discourse features aren't needed in online dialogue. In *Proceedings Association for Computational Linguistics*. Philadelphia, 19–22 June. Pp. 87–90.

Zarmer, C. (1991). ACEKit: An application construction toolkit. Report HPL-91-134. Palo Alto: Hewlett-Packard Laboratories.

Zarmer, C. and Chew, C. (1992). Frameworks for interactive, extensible, information-intensive applications. In *Proceedings UIST '92*. Monterey, CA, 15–18 November.

Zarmer, C., Nardi B., Johnson, J. and Miller, J. (1992). ACE: Zen and the art of application building. In *Proceedings of the Twenty-fifth Hawaii International Conference on System Sciences*, Koloa, HI, 7–10 January, vol. 2, pp. 687–698.

Zhang, J. (1990). The interaction of internal and external information in a problem solving task. *UCSD Technical Report #9005*. La Jolla, CA: University of California, Department of Cognitive Science.

Zloof, M. (1981). QBE/OBE: A language for office and business automation. *IEEE Computer*, May. Pp. 13–22.

Index

.